KENT'S STRANGEST TALES

Extraordinary but true stories from a
very curious county

MARTIN LATHAM

PORTICO

Published in the United Kingdom in 2016 by
Portico
1 Gower Street
London
WC1E 6HD

An imprint of Pavilion Books Company Ltd

Map credit: Map of Kent © Batsford Books

Illustrations by Matthew Booker

ISBN 978-1-91023-297-2

A CIP catalogue record for this book is available from the British Library.

10 9 8 7 6 5 4 3 2 1

Reproduction by ColourDepth UK
Printed and bound by Bookwell, Finland

This book can be ordered direct from the publisher at www.pavilionbooks.com

CONTENTS

Thames Estuary

ISLE
OF
GRAIN

Cliffe
Cooling
High Halstow
Dartford
Greenhithe
GRAVESEND
Higham Sta
Swanscombe
Chalk
Wilmington
Darenth
Medway
Sutton
S. Darenth
Cobham
Strood
ROCHESTER
Swanley
at Hone
Horton Kirby
Luddesdown
Gillingham
Upchurch
Crockenhill
Farningham
Chelsfield
Fawkham Green
Borstal
Chatham
Lower Ha
Green Street
Eynsford
Meopham
Newington
Mi
Green
Ash
Wouldham
Regis
Lullingstone
Harvel
Hartlip
Borden
Castle
Stansted
Burham
Shoreham
Fairseat
Trottiscliffe
Kit's Coty Ho.
Stockbury
Cudham
Otford
Birling
Bicknor
Mils
Knockholt
Kemsing
Wrotham
Ryarsh
Aylesford
Chevening
Dunton Green
Offham
Detling
Hucking
Fri
Sundridge
Ightham
Borough
West
MAIDSTONE
Westerham
Brasted
SEVENOAKS
Green
Malling
Bearsted
Hollingbou
Ivy Hatch
Wateringbury
Leeds
Chartwell
Ide Hill
Plaxtol
Harrietsh
Knole Park
Shipbourne
Boughton
Langley
Lenhan
Crockham
Toy's Hill
West Peckham
Mereworth
Yalding
Green
Ulcombe
Hill
Hadlow
East Peckham
Hunton
Linton
Sutton
Boughto
Edenbridge
TONBRIDGE
Golden
Chart
Valence
Malher
Leigh
Green
Medway
Laddingford
Chainhurst
Sutton
Chiddingstone
Tudeley
Collier Street
Headcorn
Hever
Marden
Plu
Penshurst
Staplehurst
Smarde
Cowden
Southborough
Brenchley
Speldhurst
Matfield
Frittenden
TUNBRIDGE
Horsmonden
WELLS
Biddenden
Goudhurst
Sissinghurst
High Hal
Lamberhurst
Cranbrook
Tenter
Gill's Green
Benenden
SUSSEX
Iden Green
Rolvenden
Hawkhurst
Dingleden
Small H
ISI
Sandhurst
Ox
Newenden
Witttersh

10

2

KENT

NORTH SEA

erness
Minster
nborough
Eastchurch
Warden
Leysdown
LE OF SHEPPEY
NGBOURNE
Whitstable
Seasalter
HERNE BAY
Reculver
Hillborough
Herne
Hoath
Chislet
Sarre
Upstreet
Monkton
Graveney
Luddenham
Oare
Dargate
Faversham
ynham
eet
Ospringe
Hernhill
Boughton
Street
Sheldwich
Selling
Throwley Forstal
Thanington
nham
astling
Blean
Sturry
W. Stourmouth
Westbere
Fordwich
CANTERBURY
Littlebourne
Chartham
Patrixbourne
Old Wives
Lees
Bekesbourne
Lower Hardres
Petham
Solestreet
Bishopsbourne
Upper
Hardres
Badlesmere
Chilham
Otterden
Stalisfield
Green
Godmersham
Charing
ng Heath
Eastwell
Court
Crundale
Boughton Lees
Westwell
Kennington
Wye
Waltham
Stelling
Minnis
Elmsted
Hastingleigh
Brook
Hinxhill
Rhodes
Minnis
Brabourne
Stowting
Chart
ASHFORD
Chart
thersden
Mersham
Smeeth
Sellindge
Bonnington
Aldington
Lympne
odchurch
Bilsington
rdington
Warehorne
Newchurch
Snave
pledore
Snargate
Brenzett
Ivychurch
ROMNEY
MARSH
Dymchurch
Brookland
Old
Romney
New Romney
WALLAND
MARSH
Lydd
Dungeness

MARGATE
Dent-de-Lion
Acol
ISLE
OF
THANET
Broadstairs
RAMSGATE
Pegwell
Minster
Stour
E. Stourmouth
Preston
Elmstone
Ebbsfleet Ho.
Richborough Castle
Wickhambreux
Wingham
Ash
Sandwich
Staple
Woodnesborough
Adisham
Worth
Eastry
Chillenden
Betteshanger
Barham
Tilmanstone
Mongeham
Deal
Welmer
Barfreston
Eythorne
Sutton
Kingsdown
Denton
W. Langdon
Ringwould
Wootton
Lydden
St Margaret's at Cliffe
Elham
Swingfield
Guston
Acrise
Ewell Minnis
St Margaret's
Bay
Lyminge
Alkham
DOVER
Hougham
Postling
Capel le
Ferne
Paddlesworth
Westenhanger
Saltwood
FOLKESTONE
Royal Military Canal
Hythe
Sandgate
Burmarsh

STRAIT OF DOVER

0   5   10   15
miles

11

INTRODUCTION

I think I enjoyed wonders too much to write a good PhD. As my excellent supervisor Peter Marshall said, I kept 'wandering off' into chatty stories. In this book I can indulge my passion for history as told by tales. I hope Professor Marshall will put a copy in his lavatory. Indeed, the smallest room is a good place for this book in any home, as there are tales to suit any length of stay.

I am a Londoner who, in 20 years of Canterbury bookselling, has fallen in love with Kent's wonders. I hope you enjoy dipping into this book, as I have loved writing it. The interwar poet Richard Church said that, while writing his book on Kent, he developed a 'mystical relationship' with the place. I might not claim that, but it has become, for me, as enchanted as Samarkand.

What a county! Nightingales haunt ancient woods, the marsh birds are internationally important, otters breed, seals bask in secret coastal nooks, and peregrine falcons speed through the air. The 'garden of England' sounds so cosy, but the garden has been dotted with chairs from which writers blew our minds: Darwin and Dickens, H.G. Wells, Joseph Conrad and T.S. Eliot all wrote their masterpieces here. Its sinuous flints stirred Henry Moore to sculpt a new humanity, and its glorious storms helped inspire Van Gogh and Turner to transform painting.

Turner once said that the light over East Kent beat anything in Italy.

This county of Kent, lying between London and Europe, can never be dull or parochial. Caesar fought woad-painted tribesmen here, and marauding Vikings felled an Archbishop of Canterbury with an ox bone. In medieval times, the port of Romney survived on importing wine and garlic. Along Kent's northern shore, Pocahontas died, Nelson's ships were built and Sir John Franklin set sail on his doomed expedition to discover the Northwest Passage. To the east, German destroyers shelled Broadstairs in the Great War, and the Luftwaffe pounded the whole county in the Second World War. Incoming trucks at Dover hide illegal immigrants from as far away as Afghanistan, and the county has its own vigorous criminal class. Kent invented chavs; they come from Chatham.

I have included myths, nature and some paranormal tales, because they too are Kent's story. As Coleridge pointed out when lamenting that Wordsworth did not believe in fairies, we cannot live only on 'matter-of-factness'.[1]

Most of all, I hope you enjoy discovering the more obscure individuals as much as I have loved unearthing them. I do not believe that any novelist would dare to portray the bounders, narcissists, losers, fantasists, nutters and quiet heroes who abound in these pages. So, to quote Evelyn Waugh's preface to Eric Newby's *A Short Walk in the Hindu Kush*: 'Dear Reader, if you have any softness left for the idiosyncrasies of our rough island race, fall to and enjoy this.'

Thanks to two kind and inspiring friends: Professor Peter Marshall, who taught me to research, and the late Dr Katherine Wyndham, who inspired me to write history and climbed trees with me. The quality of my knowledge has been much improved by many conversations with Dr Paul

1. Coleridge is quoted in Duncan Wu, *William Hazlitt, the First Modern Man* (Oxford University Press, 2008)

Bennett, Director of the Canterbury Archaeological Trust, and with his predecessor, Tim Tatton-Brown. The County Archaeologist, John Williams, urbanely answered queries. The late scholar Simon St Clair Terry understood Kent better than anyone I have met, and he gave of his erudition freely, and often hilariously. Likewise, the late Alan Clark inspired my history-writing by verbal encouragement, and I regret that I never took up his offer to write the history of Saltwood Castle. Sissinghurst features rather largely in the book, because the late Nigel Nicolson repeatedly agreed to my requests to give talks in my bookshop about the house, and about his parents Vita and Harold. I must thank Tim Waterstone for giving me the best workplace I can imagine, and asking me to make it 'an Aladdin's cave of books'.

The Keeper of Prehistoric Antiquities at the British Museum answered many queries and John Badmin, doyen of the Kent Field Club, kindly told me about Kent's natural wonders. Folkestone Tourist Office helped me to track Samuel Beckett's movements in the town, and Deal's inimitable Town Clerk, Linda Dykes, helped with Turner in Kent.

At my publishers – previously Anova, now Pavilion – Polly's faith in me was very heartening, while Malcolm Croft was a gentle polymath with a rapier wit. My thanks to Katie Cowan and Nicola Newman for the opportunity to collaborate on a new edition, and to Victoria Nairn and Katie Hewett for bringing it to fruition. Thank you to my children: Ailsa for a wise and listening ear, Oliver for keeping the tales readable (and supplying two), India for enthusiasm when I doubted, Caspar for being Horatio when I was a dithering Hamlet, and William for verbal virtuosity. My stepchildren have endured my rambling anecdotes; Francesca, Jack and Sam – thanks. My wife Claire is a fantastic editor who saved the reader from many verbal infelicities, and secured my felicity throughout.

Martin Latham

Kent ... sweet is the country, because full of riches

(*William Skakespeare*, Henry VI,
Part II, *Act IV, Scene VII*)

BRITAIN'S OLDEST HIGHWAY?

600,000 BC

The North Downs, as you can see by looking across the Channel, are mirrored by chalk cliffs in the Pas de Calais. The English Channel was created about 400,000 years ago. Before that, there was a land bridge to the continent, from Calais to Dover. 'Bipedal hominids', as archaeologists romantically call the early prototypes of mankind, originated in Africa's Rift Valley and spread to Europe over a million years ago. Their entry route into England was along the Calais–Dover chalk ridge, continuing inland along the North Downs.

Kent was Early Man's bridgehead into Britain. Our primitive ancestors crossed the chalk land bridge to Dover and fanned out. Evidently, many colonists remained in Kent, for one archaeologist has called it 'the richest county in England' for evidence of prehistoric man. So far, an exceptional 40,000 artefacts have been found from this ancient influx.

Ornithologists still report that this remains an ancient 'avian highway', a route used by many migratory birds into England. They are following our early ancestors. This intercontinental highway has continued in use by birds and man for millennia.

Down it has flowed a veritable pageant of English history. Henry VIII took it in 1520 to meet the King of France on the Field of the Cloth of Gold. In 1660, Charles II returned from the Hague to London and a coronation via the A2 route. At the end of Mozart's triumphant 1764–5 visit to England, his coach went down the Dover Road A2, pausing to inspect army manoeuvres at Barham Downs. The railway, built in 1861, follows the chalk ridge to Dover port as well. In 1884, when Gordon of Khartoum was sent on his doomed expedition to the Sudan, he took the Boat Train to Dover. The Prime Minister, William Gladstone, said farewell at Victoria Station. Millions of soldiers in two World Wars took the route. In 1948, a runner carried the Olympic torch, kindled in Athens, from Dover to the Olympiad in London. In *The Italian Job,* Michael Caine's coachload of villains descends the then-futuristic curving flyover to Dover docks, en route to Milan. One transport historian has confidently called the A2 route 'the oldest highway in Britain', and it is one of the oldest in Europe. It is still in use, day and night. Via this route, Kent is Britain's gateway to the rest of the world and this accounts for many of the strangest tales in this book. Kent is known as the Garden of England, but it has always been a very exotic, cosmopolitan patch.

SUNNY SPELL, WITH GIANT ELEPHANTS

400,000 BC

Climate change in Kent has been drastic and has led to many strange and curious discoveries. Around 400,000 BC, there was a warm, wet period of 45,000 years, between two Ice Ages. Rhinos and buffaloes flourished and an unusual biped shared their world: the earliest humans in England. In 1935, Alvan Marston, a dentist with an interest in the Palaeolithic, noticed skull fragments in a quarry at Swanscombe, in northwest Kent. He knew there was something unusual about the jaw structure, and informed the British Museum, who ignored him. He hunted on every weekend, undeterred, and, nine months later, he had an almost incredible find: a second piece of the same skull. This brought the Museum staff down to Swanscombe. Twenty years later, 80ft (24.4m) away, an archaeologist found the final piece of skull. Swanscombe Man, as the remains became known, was a find of international importance, an ancestor of *Homo sapiens* known, cumbersomely, as *Homo heidelbergensis* (he was first found near Heidelberg in Germany).

No clothes have been found with this early version of mankind, so it's thought that he had a pelt of fur, or a good padding of fat. One archaeologist asks us to imagine them as a race of rugby internationals 7ft (2.1m) tall!

Their prey was equally impressive, as the builders of the new Ebbsfleet Station, near Swanscombe, discovered in

2004. They stumbled upon the skeleton of a giant elephant, the size of a double-decker bus, lying in mud at the edge of what had been a prehistoric lake. To the amazement of archaeologists, it was surrounded by flint tools: it had been felled by those early, pugnacious Kentish people, using their wooden spears. Having no skill with fire, they ate such meat raw. The fact that they did not have language increases the impression of beast-like creatures, but this is far from the truth. Swanscombe Man's skull indicates a large brain, and the skull's ear structure indicates that these people communicated by sound. Dogs communicate with man, but not each other, by intonations, because they, amazingly, recognise how much we still convey by pitch and tone. Recent discoveries among Amazonian tribes, some of whom communicate in wordless song, have led to the widely accepted 'Singing Neanderthal' theory. Music predated language, and it seems that these incredibly tough human ancestors communicated with each other in 'musilanguage'.[1]

As you park at Ebbsfleet – the elephant was under the car park – you can take your imagination on an excursion and see our tall, robust ancestors, hunting in groups, intoning to each other with expressive head movements and hand gestures, and occasionally laughing. Laughter, that uniquely human thing, appears to have predated language too.

1. A term coined by Stephen Mithen. See his *Singing Neanderthals* (Phoenix, London, 2005)

HOW A NEW GUINEA TRIBE SOLVED A KENT MYSTERY

4000 BC

A mysterious polished axe-head was discovered near Canterbury in Victorian times. The axe-head, dated to 4000 BC, was given to the British Museum by a Major Frank Goldney in 1901. It was one of the landmark artefacts featured in Radio 4's *A History of the World in 100 Objects*. Extraordinarily beautiful, it is made of highly polished jade. This exotic opaque green stone is not found in Britain. Moreover, the axe was so perfectly polished, with its edges intact, that it was clearly made never to be used, a magical object. In remote parts of Spain today, peasants still rub jade on their body to cure a range of illnesses. Our strange tale now moves to a fog-haunted mountain village on the French–Swiss border. It was here, in the 1960s, that an 18-year-old called Pierre Petrequin made a remarkable discovery. A keen potholer, he found in an alpine cave a complete prehistoric kitchen, left so intact with pots, hearth and implements that it might have just been deserted the day before. This drew him into a lifelong career as an archaeologist with a deep understanding of European tribal life. He met a local girl, Anne-Marie, who had grown up like Heidi, tending mountain flocks all summer. As narrated by a French newspaper profile, Anne-Marie had a quiet smile and loved to hear Pierre's tales of Stone Age man. They married in the 70s, and both found jobs at the archaeology institute down in the valley, at Besançon, eastern France.

The Petrequins wanted to understand Europe's tribal past; their own personal histories made them feel closer to that past than many an urbanite academic. So they went to Papua New Guinea, one of the last places on earth where mankind still makes stone axes. There they were intrigued to find elegant stone axe-heads in the tacky little market-town of Jayapura. Enquiring after their source, the couple were directed to the mountain community of Yelema. The heat and the arduous climb made both Pierre and Anne-Marie seriously ill, and they found the Yelema people completely unused to the sight of white Europeans. But the trip paid off, and the Petrequins learned that axe-heads made at high altitude have a special magical significance, being used in a range of rituals. On their return to Besançon they became fascinated with the mystery of the Kent jade axe. Perhaps it too came from some European mountain version of Yelema? The quest took them 12 years and involved some state-of-the-art petrographic analysis, but, unbelievably, they found the very block of jadeite that the Kent axe came from, high in the Italian Alps. Hollow scars in the block, made by the ancient quarrymen, with chips littered below, provided satisfying confirmation of their discovery.

Bizarrely, the Petrequins found that there was no need to quarry jade at such high altitude; excellent jade could be found low down at the foot of the alps. There is only one conclusion: ritual axes like this derive part of their magic from their source, the high mountain places which are so important in every spiritual system, be it Hinduism or Christianity, Buddhism or *Lord of the Rings*. As British Museum Director Neil MacGregor (writer and presenter of the Radio 4 series) put it, 'The jade-seekers chose this special spot, with spectacular vistas stretching as far as the eye can see, in a place midway between our world on earth and the realm of gods.'

PARTYING
WITH THE DEAD
c.2000 BC

Kent's eastern spur, the Isle of Thanet, has an extraordinary light. The renowned landscape painter J.M.W. Turner, who painted there a lot, said it was better than anything in Italy. Forget the cabbages and the flatness, and just *feel* the atmosphere. In Stone Age times, it was full of barrows, causeways, sacred circles and strange rituals. Ploughing has destroyed most of the evidence but Thanet was, as Deputy Director of the Canterbury Archaeological Trust Peter Clark says, 'part of a huge monumental landscape comparable to Wessex [the Stonehenge landscape]'. The rituals, it is becoming clear, were probably the strangest-ever happenings in Kent. They remain utterly mysterious to us, which means that, enjoyably, your guess is as good as any archaeologist's. Why, for instance, are carved chalk phalluses found with chalk rings which, Clark's team conclude coyly, 'refer to female sexuality'?

Then there is the 10-metre-diameter circle of banked earth at North Foreland. It had spectacular views over the sea and, with its narrow entrance, was used for ... who knows? Dancing? Praying? A teenage girl was buried there in a crouched position. She was covered by a large flat piece of whalebone. Academics report these facts baldly, without interpretation, but the imagination is fired. The critically acclaimed Maori film *Whale Rider*, about a 12-year-old girl's rediscovery of her people's whale myths, comes to mind, as does the sacred use of whalebone by dowsers.

Monkton, near Ramsgate, was another sacred burial site, extensive and in use for hundreds of years. Here excarnation was practised, that is, the ritual of removing flesh from the bones of the dead. Skeletons were 'disarticulated' in multiple excarnations, i.e. important bones and skulls were mixed together for ritual use. This was done in large, purpose-built buildings, which commanded fine views, in a party atmosphere. It all sounds like a bad horror movie, but excarnation has been practised by Tibetans, Zoroastrians and Comanche Indians.

This idea became easier to handle in 2011 when New York historian Erik Seeman wrote *The Huron-Wendat Feast of the Dead*. A Canadian tribe, the Huron-Wendat, were still partying with bones in 1636. They invited Jean de Brebeuf, a Catholic priest from Normandy who spoke Huron-Wendat, to their Feast. As Seeman says, 'Although a modern American would be disgusted and perplexed by the elaborate ceremonies centred on human bones', seventeenth-century Europeans saw a lot of death at first hand, and Catholics were very comfortable with the idea of holy bones. Brebeuf loved the Feast, which demonstrated great devotion and love towards 'the residents of the spirit world'. Moreover, the bone parties had a message for the living. As another priest noted, 'by means of these ceremonies they make new friendships among themselves, saying that, just as the bones of their friends and family are united, so they ought to live in the same unity and harmony'. Drumming and chanting, Brebeuf wrote, brought participants into a trance-like state of communion with their ancestors. At the end of the Feast, men and women carried relatives' bones to a burial pit to re-inter them. They carefully unwrapped them from beaver skins, wrote a spectator, 'with tears streaming down their cheeks' and said their final farewell. Brebeuf was particularly moved by one woman whose father had died. 'She handled his bones, one after another, with much affection.'

We may never know much about Thanet's feasts of the dead, but, next time you are driving to Broadstairs, or perhaps visiting the Westwood Cross shopping centre, it might be interesting to bear in mind that, as archaeologist Peter Clark drily observes, 'burial practices in Thanet were far more intricate and multifarious than we had previously envisaged'.

KENT'S MOST ENCHANTED ROOM

80 AD

Nowadays most people who live around Sevenoaks perform a daily commute to London. Many work in the financial sector or the civil service. Two thousand years ago, a 66-year-old Italian got up in the morning and left his suburban villa to take up a rather different job: Governor of the Roman Empire in Africa. Two years later he became the nineteenth Emperor of Rome and soon after that, a god.

Pertinax was a grizzled career soldier and ex-slave, a commander loved by his men and famed for victorious campaigns in Persia and Romania, Bulgaria and Germany. Described as rotund, but always with a regal bearing, he had been Governor of Syria and Governor of Britain. There are echoes here of the Russell Crowe character in *Gladiator*, and the parallel becomes even closer, for Pertinax succeeded the voluptuously cruel Emperor Commodus (played in the film by Joaquin Phoenix). Emperor Pertinax sold off Commodus' more extreme luxuries: the golden chariots, the legions of prostitutes (male and female). He ended orgiastic banquets – gaining ridicule by championing, among other wild foods, edible thistles – paid both army back pay and nine years of outstanding poor relief. He reformed the Imperial currency and curbed the use of the death penalty.

What a mysterious mixture Pertinax was: a radical reformer who sentimentally kept his father's old haberdashery shop open in Rome and a fierce disciplinarian who loved to have poetry read to him. His idea of a good evening was dinner with a few friends and conversation about books – he had been a teacher before joining the army. But the most remarkable evidence of his complexity was discovered here, south of Sevenoaks, in 1952, by another veteran soldier.

Colonel Geoffrey Meates was a balding and bespectacled Philip Larkin lookalike. (This description was provided by a customer in my bookshop who was present at the excavation 55 years ago.) He had served with distinction in India, at Dunkirk and during the Nazi siege of Malta. In his Kentish retirement he took up archaeology and was lucky enough to direct the excavation of Lullingstone Villa, now known to be the house of Pertinax. The whole discovery started when a farm labourer drove a fence post through a mosaic and Meates spent eight years excavating Lullingstone.

Pertinax had taken over a smaller villa on rising ground overlooking the River Darent. Darent means 'clear water' and the river rises clear from the chalk below. The intimate secluded valley of this Thames tributary still has a mystical atmosphere. Pre-Roman pagan locals felt it; they revered three water nymphs at Lullingstone. The Celts felt it, naming the area 'place of running water in the oaks'. It was the 'valley of vision' for the nineteenth-century painter Samuel Palmer, who lived there in a ramshackle cottage.

Pertinax felt it too. He extended the house into a double-winged villa with a long verandah overlooking the river. And this tough soldier respected the local deities, in a very unmodern way. Romans believed, as did their Britannic subjects, in deities throughout the natural world. Every wood or spring might have a 'genius loci' or 'spirit of the place'. The Romans in Britain did not think it was inconsistent to simply add these native deities to their Mediterranean pantheon. It was akin to today's 'basic Health and Safety'. In a world still magical, why not hedge your bets? The Lullingstone guidebook calls it 'pragmatic polytheism'.

Pertinax built a bathhouse, with a public entrance, so that locals could benefit from the waters of a spring, which rose under his house and fed the Darent. As for the cellar with a well in the floor containing the spring, this was turned into an underground temple, dedicated to the three water nymphs. It could be accessed from the house above but also via a public door. In a niche a fresco was painted of the nymphs, by an Italian artist. Clear water flows from the breast of one of them.

Offerings were thrown into the well and even now villa visitors throw money despite the fact English Heritage have erected a sign saying 'Please donate offerings at the Gift Shop'. They miss the point really: perhaps we are not so very different from Pertinax and those ancient Kentish locals .

As Emperor in Rome, surely Pertinax fondly recalled the cool green Kentish valley, the balconied house where he had hoped to take early retirement, and the sacred peace of his nymphaeum. Sadly his uprightness and economies made enemies among Commodus' cronies, who murdered him and put his head on a pole in the Forum.

The three nymphs lived on. Their appeal was so enduring that, even when a Christian house-chapel was installed 300 years later, the 'Deep Room' continued in ritual use, accessed via a trapdoor and ladder. (Worshippers going down there mirrored Jung's twentieth-century dreams of going down a cellar ladder to access the collective unconscious.)

Eventually, as the Roman Empire declined, the nymph shrine in the basement became unfashionable. The Deep Room was whitewashed and a bust of the deified Pertinax was placed there until it was discovered by Colonel Meates. The niche with the marvellous fresco of nymphs became a handy cupboard. A shelf was added, right across the middle, but the builder doing the job seems to have had a heart: told to plaster over the nymph frescoes in the niche, he carefully made a partition in front of them, without actually slapping plaster onto them. Thanks to the sentimental action of one person, two millennia ago, we have this glimpse of an ancient, nature-worshipping Kent, of magical thinking a mile from Sevenoaks.

THE MYSTERY TEMPLE ON THE MARSH

c.80 AD

The village of Stone on Romney Marsh is, my 1881 guidebook says, 'in a somewhat unfrequented corner of Kent', and even today it feels far from anywhere. With its lonely red telephone box and fine old church surrounded by a huddle of ancient buildings, it is a vision of traditional Englishness (indeed, the late Sir Donald Sinden, so quintessentially English, lived in the village next door).

But in the church is something exotic, Mediterranean and unique in all of Britain, something after which the village is named: a large stone Roman altar, 2 sq. ft (0.2 sq. m) and nearly 4ft (1.2m) tall. It has frequently been banished as a pagan nightmare, to a local farmyard, and then to the vicarage garden. The fine carved bull's heads on each face are conclusive evidence that this altar was part of a temple to Mithras which was on this site. Mithras was a god of Persian origins, much worshipped by Roman soldiers.

What exactly were the rites of Mithras? Victorian scholars predictably hinted at sacrifice, pointing to the iron ring in the altar: surely used to secure the screaming victim? Not quite, it was put there by the local farmer when he used the stone to tie up horses.

Although past fantasies of bulls being slaughtered and virgins sacrificed have evaporated, the truth is even stranger. In Mithraism, naked initiates drank a sacred drink (similar to the Brahmins' ritual soma and the Christians' communion wine) and after ceremonially smashing the vessel, were guided, using breathing exercises and chanting, towards a state of *eudaimonia*, which is variously translated as happiness or profound content.

So, a returning Roman soldier sailing down the Channel one night in a galley, on his way home perhaps, would see the Roman lighthouse or *pharos* at Dover comfortingly blazing (it's still the biggest Roman building left in Britain), then the cliff-top villas and bath-houses of Folkestone, followed by the large Roman fort on the hill at Lympne, and finally, as he left the Dover Straits going south, the little Oxney, temple to Mithras, a place of ritual which had given heat, warmth and a sense of profound wellbeing to relieve the tour of duty on Britannia, that dangerous, rain-sodden land.

WHY THE HORSESHOE
IS LUCKY

c.980 AD

Nobody has heard of St Dunstan these days, but this Archbishop of Canterbury was England's best-loved saint before the whole fuss of Thomas Becket eclipsed him. (He is not even in the index of the recent comprehensive book *Canterbury, 2000 Years of History*.) People loved him, singing songs and chanting rhymes about him, but the main reminder of his popularity is the many churches named after him. In Anglo-Saxon times, before the French takeover in 1066, he was to us what the current Dalai Lama is to Tibetans, a man of genuine holiness. The more one reads of Dunstan, the more attractive he becomes, whereas the reverse happens when you study ego-mad, scheming Becket.

Dunstan was really a monk all his life. A Wessex boy, he loved learning and prayer from an early age, but always wanted to be useful to the world too. So he was a keen musician, an accomplished manuscript scribe and a good artist. His charming self-portrait, doodled in a margin, is at the Bodleian Library in Oxford. As an accomplished silversmith and blacksmith, he is the patron saint of those trades. Popular as a trusted adviser, he was close to successive kings. In 955, when he found the dissolute young King Eadwig enjoying a cross-generational threesome with a noblewoman and her mother, Dunstan reproved the King and made a tactical retreat to Belgium (Flanders, as it then was). While there, he was inspired by the practices of the Benedictine monks at Ghent, practices which he brought back to England after Eadwig's death in 959. The new King, Edgar the Peaceful, appointed Dunstan Archbishop of Canterbury.

Although he held this post for 18 years, and reformed English monasteries along purer, Benedictine lines, his retirement in Canterbury is more interesting. For ten years, up to his death, he was a simple monk again, spending long hours in prayer and mystical exploration, teaching, playing music, manuscript-making and working with metal. He even learned, in retirement, how to make bells.

Throughout his life, Dunstan had an intimate relationship with 'discarnate entities', both good and evil. Early on, rival monks threw him into a cesspit, suspecting him of witchcraft. In later years, the devil had burst into his cell to stop him playing the harp. One day in Canterbury, the story goes, the devil, knowing Dunstan's skill as a blacksmith, asked him to shoe his hooves. Knowing who his customer was, Dunstan drove a nail into the flesh of the devil's foot. The roaring was heard for miles, but Dunstan only removed the nail when the devil agreed that he would never enter a house with a horseshoe over the door. Thus, Dunstan provided the English householder thereafter with a cheap, simple way to repel Beelzebub. Lord Nelson even nailed a horseshoe to the mast of HMS *Victory*. Angels frequently appeared to Dunstan too, and their singing inspired his music. In 988, they appeared to him in Canterbury to predict his death in three days' time. He gave a sermon telling the congregation that he was about to die, chose his burial spot, retired to bed and died peacefully on day three.

THE WORLD RECORD FOR THE LAVATORY LONGEST IN USE

1085–1948

And this isn't the *only* plumbing wonder in Canterbury. In 1155, less than a hundred years after the Battle of Hastings, Prior Wilbert engineered a sophisticated water supply system for the monks of Canterbury, based on Ancient Roman practice. He brought fresh water from springs half a mile (0.8km) away, using hydraulics and a water tower (still visible in the cathedral precincts) to maintain pressure. On the hill where the springs are, a large conduit-house, excavated late in the twentieth century, is now a seldom-visited English Heritage site, incongruously set in a modern housing estate. In the cathedral precincts, an extraordinary system of pipes snaked through the monks' dormitory, wash-house and vegetable garden. Most pipes were lead, with some made from elm wood, chosen for its water-resistance.

We know so much about this system for two reasons. Firstly, Edwine, a medieval monk with perhaps too much time on his hands, made an elaborate drawing of the water system in his prayer book. Secondly, until about 1990, the cathedral gardeners were still using the system to water their plants, 800 years on. In 1995, Paul Bennett, Director of the Canterbury Archaeological Trust, restored the pipework. When he opened the valves fully, he flooded the cathedral precincts with spring-water. Much to his understandable annoyance, Canterbury Council subsequently allowed roadworks to break up the water system irrevocably.

Back to the lavatory. William the Conqueror appointed Lanfranc, a brilliant Italian, as his Archbishop of Canterbury. Born in the late 900s or early 1000s, Lanfranc was already a wise old thinker, with a reputation for philosophy and theology (a future Pope was among his pupils). Despite this lofty monastic background, he took to politics and the affairs of the world very effectively, becoming King William's deputy; he even ran the country when William was away. But his Christianity remained strong, fuelled by a vow to do good works which he made in France, when muggers beat him up and left him tied to a tree. This philanthropy found expression in the establishment of several 'hospitals', or poor-houses, in Kent. Most of them survive today as charitable old people's homes. One of these, St John's Hospital, hidden away near Sainsbury's supermarket in Canterbury, had a separate toilet block, built in 1085. The block remained in use until 1948, for nearly a thousand years. Imagine! Almshouse residents in successive dress styles must have sat in there while the Battle of Agincourt raged, the Taj Mahal was built, *Hamlet* was staged for the first time, Charles I was beheaded, the French Revolution unfolded, the British Empire rose and fell, the Battle of the Somme ended a million men's lives and Hitler took on the world. As the Battle of Britain thrillingly unfolded over Kent's summer skies, residents sat in the cool building, with its 2ft (0.6m) thick flint walls. People popped in and out on the day that Britain handed India its independence. Soon afterwards, perhaps someone took a newspaper into one of the ancient lavatories and read about Gandhi's assassination. This toilet block, built just after the Norman Conquest by order of Lanfranc, provided peaceful interludes to its users for centuries. In 1948, the lavatories were finally decommissioned, but, by appointment with the residents, you can still visit them.

THE SIAMESE TWINS OF BIDDENDEN

c.1100

The mysteries surrounding these sisters are as intriguing as the pair themselves. Did they even exist? This is one of those unusual cases where scepticism about a folk story has decreased in modern time, as more true cases of Siamese twins come to light. Edward Hasted, an influential eighteenth-century Kent historian, dismissed the Biddenden twins as a folk myth, partly because he had no experience of such cases. He was one of those people – we have all met them – who just love to be right against a majority, a know-all. Egerton Brydges, a scholar who knew Hasted, called him 'a little mean-looking man with no extraordinary qualities of mind except a good memory'. Brydges especially noted Hasted's lack of imagination. He was a left-brainer, an accumulator of facts, a gazetteer-man, an empiricist. To such people, the novel, the new, 'does not compute'.

The most famous conjoined twins are the nineteenth-century Thai brothers Chang and Eng. After touring as a circus attraction, they settled in the USA as farmers. They each married (they had a huge bed for four) and fathered, between them, 21 children. They died, much respected, within three hours of each other.

Other information has come to light since Hasted dismissed the Biddenden case. Peruvian ceramics depict conjoined twins as early as 300 AD, and a pair were documented in Constantinople in 942 AD. An unfortunate Italian pair of conjoined twins toured American circuses in the nineteenth century.

The 'Biddenden Maids', Mary and Eliza Chulkhurst, remain the earliest named Siamese twins in the world. They are thought to have lived in medieval times, though the dates are all very vague. Comfortably wealthy, they left 20 acres (8.1ha) of land to provide for an annual distribution of food to the needy of the parish. This food includes the 'Biddenden cakes', stamped with an image of the twin sisters. Images of these cakes go back to the 1770s. Fascinatingly, the cakes may also have contributed to the downgrading of the Maids from history to mythology: they appear to depict twins fully dressed, joined both at the shoulder and hip. This was virtually impossible, but modern experts point out that real Siamese twins tend to walk with their arms around each other's shoulders. Is this what the cakes depict? They seem to.

The sisters' charity still exists, and when their 20 acres – known as the Bread and Cheese Lands – were sold for housing, the funds were ploughed back into the charity. Every Easter Monday, food, including Biddenden cakes, is distributed to local widows and pensioners. And, as the years pass, Hasted's books are increasingly being seen as riddled with inaccuracies.

THE NEUROSCIENCE
OF THOMAS BECKET'S
MARTYRDOM

1170

We all have left-brain moments, when we see the world in parts, analytically, humourlessly, 'for what it is'. And we all have right-brain times, when we get 'the big picture', see our lives more poetically, romantically. By 'romantically', I mean as part of a story. At these right-brain times, we appreciate music and metaphor, dance and sensuality. Rene Descartes and Jeremy Bentham are two quintessentially left-brain philosophers. They distrusted metaphor and poetry. Both were rigid in defence of their belief system, which was materialistic more than spiritual. Both saw their bodies as objects. For them, the body was not something to 'get in touch with'. Descartes saw the body as a separate engine, a mere mechanism. He pioneered experimentation on live animals, having somehow deduced that animals cannot feel pain. He saw passers-by as automata or puppets. He was puzzled that they were unaware of their puppet-like bodies. In this he was on the same spectrum as people who have sustained right-brain damage. One such patient cut his arm to see if there was oil inside. Bentham and Descartes' attitude is underlined by the way that, at their behest, their bodies were dismembered after death. The Frenchman's was distributed around France, while Bentham's was stuffed and displayed in London.

Iain McGilchrist is a neuroscientist who sees right- and left-brain patterns in history. He can explain the traits of, say, the French Revolution (left-brain, ritual dismemberments) and Romanticism (right-brain, sensual) by reference to the dominance of one side of our brains over the other. So his book, *The Master and the Emissary* (Yale University Press, 2009), is subtitled 'The Divided Brain and the Making of the Western World'. The entire saga of Thomas Becket's murder is remarkable evidence for twelfth-century Europe being a time of left-brain dominance. We know an unusually large amount about Becket's psychology, because after his martyrdom countless biographies appeared. Anyone who knew him even slightly wrote down every detail. He was the Elvis of the Middle Ages. The Archbishop was a nit-picker, a detail freak. His uncompromising rigidity led him, on just one day, to excommunicate ten people. Such inflexibility is, to use the adjective derived from our French philosopher above, highly Cartesian. With a bit of metaphor and imagination or humour, Becket could have stepped back from his quarrel with his king, who was equally inflexible. The quarrel was an unspiritual affair, a wrangle over rights and jurisdictions. But these were left-brain times.

Even sculpture at this time was flat and stiff, with stylised faces. The body would only come to be celebrated in art 300 years later, in the Renaissance (which McGilchrist points to as a high-tide mark of right-brain dominance).

Thomas Becket, like Descartes, saw the body as a source of trouble. To subdue his sexual thoughts, he would lie in freezing streams for hours on end. To punish his appetite he lived for long periods only on water in which fennel had been boiled. To get closer to his puritanical beliefs he wore a knee-length hair shirt. This was never washed and contemporaries noted approvingly that it was crawling with lice. Some, in hushed tones, spoke admiringly of feasting maggots. He regularly submitted to flagellation to subdue and punish his body, and hinted at fantasies of dying a Christ-like death.

This was the spirit of the age. His successor-archbishop

visited a local hermit to be flogged regularly. The contemporary Crusader order, the Knights Templar, often wore a special hidden cutting blade on their leg to keep them in pain, and they worshipped the severed head of a long-dead colleague.

Further psychotic attitudes to the body emerge from an eyewitness account of Becket's murder in Canterbury Cathedral. Becket's friend Edward Grim described how, once the top of the Archbishop's head had been sliced off by a sword-blow from one of the knights, the brain and blood 'brightened the floor with the colours of the lily and the rose'. Another knight spread the brains over the pavement in a pattern. This behaviour has led some to presume the martyrdom was an occult murder but, no, it was a left-brain-style killing, with all the cold, mechanical behaviour of the right-brain-damaged psycho-killers of modern times.

When Henry II heard about the murder, which he had sort of ordered, he agonised with remorse. Who was to blame? The body, of course: he had himself flogged through Canterbury High Street, a penance which onlookers observed with approval.

Of course, mankind needs both brain hemispheres to function, but the twelfth century shows what happens when the left side dominates. Becket's martyrdom was a manifestation of such dominance. It came about because of an unimaginative rigidity, and an attitude to the body which would, thank God, change radically in the bawdy, humour-filled Renaissance.

FOR THRILL-SEEKING CAMPANOLOGISTS

1250–1820

For bell-ringers, three locations in Kent are each unique in their own way. For a campanologist, or bell-ringer if you prefer, stumbling upon any of these three places is like a philatelist finding a rare misprinted Penny Black, or a hippy finding some new magic mushroom.

First, there is Brookland, a wonderfully remote village on Romney Marsh. The Marsh was for centuries in danger of foreign invasion: marsh-dwellers have contended with Vikings and Nazi spies. The weather has been an even greater threat. The area was ravaged by an epic storm in the Middle Ages, which destroyed New Romney harbour and diverted a river into Sussex. Marsh-folk were so shaken by this catastrophe that they built, in 1250, a strange stand-alone wooden bell-tower on the raised ground of Brookland churchyard. It is a magnificent survival, 75ft (22.9m) tall, still supporting 35cwt (1,800kg) of ancient bells, and a reminder of the power that bells once had. Bell-ringing to stop storms used to be so popular that, in eighteenth-century France, 103 bell-ringers were killed by lightning in a 30-year period (wet ropes were the problem). And, because bell-ringing still signalled an invasion as late as 1940, bell-ringing was banned during the Second World War. As if to demonstrate this pre-Christian power, Brookland's tower is topped by a flying dragon weather vane.

The second head-trip for bell-ringers is in Thanet: the

Waterloo Tower in Quex Park, near Ramsgate. It was built in 1820, by a 50-year-old eccentric landowner called John Powell. Standing alone in the middle of cow pasture, it was built purely to indulge Powell's passion for campanology (he never married, and he never needed a job). The white-painted iron top section of the tower was a daring enterprise, often compared to the Eiffel Tower (built 70 years later) as a pioneering use of exposed ironwork in architecture. Enjoyably, a name has been discovered on the upper struts, not of some distinguished London engineer, but of 'John Clark'. Clark, Powell's estate manager, designed the folly himself. Even more curiously, Powell wrote a complex campanology book attempting to explain how 'Stedman Triples' could be rung: this problem was for a long time the bell-ringers' equivalent of 'Fermat's Last Theorem' in mathematics, i.e. something which could apparently never be solved. The book was privately printed, and Powell explained in a preface that it must never be sold; only given as a gift, and only to those who would truly appreciate it. To price it, he wrote, 'would be a degradation'. Neither the British Library nor the Bodleian Library has a copy. Only 20 copies have been traced worldwide, of which nine are still in Powell's library at Quex Park. He did not find many worthy recipients. Two more copies are treasured heirlooms of a family in a nearby village. Although a later expert dismissed the book as 'technically useless', it has recently been reassessed as the work of 'a real pioneer' in campanology.

The third campanological eccentricity is even more bizarrely English than the first two. Scholars flock to lonely Barfreston Church, between Canterbury and Dover, as an architectural gem, a pure Norman church with mysterious carvings. But most visitors miss something which children and children-at-heart love more than anything. Because the church is perched romantically on a hillside (which it started to slip down in Victorian times), there is no space

45

for a tower at Barfreston. Instead, the bells are hung high up in the churchyard yew tree. They are rung by a system of levers in the church, connected to the bells by aerial cables and pulleys crossing high above the churchyard. Whether the system is Heath Robinson or brilliant lateral thinking, like our other two 'unchurched' bell-towers, it works.

THE RIVER THAT LEFT KENT OVERNIGHT

1287

Romney Marsh is 100 sq. miles (259 sq. km) of strangeness. With its sparse population, winding water channels and wide skies, it has always felt unique. The Victorians called it 'The Fifth Continent'. It has abandoned villages with ruins crumbling into the mud: one is called Buttdarts, another Snave. It has invented words all of its own, words which send your imagination to soggy fens and glinting meres: 'gutts' are outfalls, such as Willop Gutt. A 'fleet' is a creek offshoot. Dunes are 'helmes', a groyne is a 'knock', a 'peat shovel' a beetle and the 'Rhee Wall' is a watercourse, or 'watergange'. Confusingly, sewers abound, but these are clean-water channels. The word originated on the marsh but was stolen by the rest of Britain for lavatorial use. Romney Marsh smugglers, known for imitating a certain bird, were 'owlers', celebrated in Russell Thorndike's *Dr Syn* books and films, and by Kipling:

If you wake at midnight, and hear a horse's feet,
Don't go drawing back the blind, or looking in the street,
Them that ask no questions isn't told a lie.
Watch the wall, my darling, while the Gentlemen go by!

Five and twenty ponies, trotting through the dark
Brandy for the parson, Baccy for the Clerk;
Laces for a Lady, Letters for a Spy,
And watch the wall, my darling, while the Gentlemen go by.

As a Canterbury bookshop manager, I once received a sick-note from a marsh-dweller with 'marsh ague' written on it. Although bogus, I accepted it, out of admiration for the *chutzpah* of this marsh-man. Marsh ague, long extinct, was a virulent malaria associated with the aggressive marsh mosquitoes. St Anselm of Canterbury tried to cure a medieval case.

Out on the Marsh, even today, Nature rules. Apart from mosquitoes, mammal-sucking leeches may attach themselves to your dog, should Fido go for a splash in the creek. The original Marsh Mallow still grows, much to the relief of the rare Marsh Mallow Moth, which has only one other UK habitat. Residents are kept awake by the Laughing Frog, and on walks they might see insects struggling for life on the carnivorous Nottingham Catchfly plant (extinct for many a year in Nottinghamshire). There is an endangered butterfly, the wonderfully named Grizzled Skipper. The Water Parsnip, the Wild Carrot, a dramatic-looking Flowering Rush which astonished me as a holidaying teenager out on my bicycle, these are just a few of the wild wonders of this strange land. Even the sheep are special: bred there since Saxon times on the highly fertile alluvial fields, they can resist foot-rot and are highly prized. Almost every sheep in Australia is descended from Marsh ancestors.

Romney was the Marsh port for centuries, its harbour formed by the mouth of the River Rother. This trading route went back a long way: a hard-to-imagine fleet of 250 Viking ships went pillaging up the River Rother in 892. In the Middle Ages, exotic imports were unloaded at Romney, especially garlic and wine. Ships tied up to iron hooks on the churchyard wall.

Then, one night in 1287, the 'storm of storms' roared on to the Marsh. Even the medieval chroniclers' habitual powers of exaggeration could not do it justice. 'The sea yielded such a roaring that it was heard a great distance inland', the moon was tinged red, ships were broken to matchwood, and the whole of nearby Old Winchelsea was destroyed. In Romney, 4ft (1.2m) of shingle and sand surged into the town so that, to this day, the street level is higher, and many old houses, like the church, have steps down to their front doors. Worst of all, residents stepped out of their battered houses to an incredible scene. The Rother had simply gone. The tempest had changed the river's course so that it now ran into the sea at Rye in Sussex.

Romney residents worked all day to dig a channel along which the Rother might be coaxed back, but it had left for ever. Romney's prosperity declined and Rye flourished (although, through silting up, it too is now far from the sea).

To this day, you can see the hooks on the churchyard wall where medieval ships from far and wide tied up, in the glory days of Romney Harbour.

THE TROUBLESOME CHURCH

1326–1954

The Isle of Sheppey is ancient, mysterious and mostly deserted, a wonderful place to visit. The storm-battered caravans and menacing old prison only add to the otherworldly atmosphere. It is unique in Kent and in the world. Its wide lonely marshes, home of the densest Wader population in the country, are fiercely protected by the RSPB. Visitors sometimes report UFOs, mistaking the amazing morphing, swirling flocks of curlew for alien craft. The isle is a fossil-hunters' mecca: elephants, crocodiles and turtles have all left their remains in the cliffs. I recall easily picking up fossilised sharks' teeth on holiday in the late 1950s (under my dad's guidance).

There is talk of a Druid fire shrine. The Romans built a temple to Apollo, a site which the Saxons reused to worship Thor. Vikings invaded often. Saxon times seem to have been a high point on the island. A Californian historian went to study Sheppey society in 1998. She found it so undisturbed that, while mums in other deprived parts of the UK were shouting 'Come 'ere, Chardonnay!' (or Wayne), on Sheppey they shouted 'Come 'ere, Egbert!' (or Sexburga). Saxon names survived. The first bridge to Sheppey was only built in 1906.

And local place-names resonate like curlew calls. Ships which manage to avoid Dead Man's Island might ground on the Horse Sands, take a wrong turning into Cockleshell

Creek or, worse still, enter the South Deep, a cul-de-sac channel in a mud plateau. Nobody lives on Dutchman's Island, a peninsular so boggily inaccessible that the RSPB don't even need to protect it. 'Scrapes' are marshy pools. 'Cotterels' are the amazing Silbury-shaped mounds which dot the isle. All theories about them are unconvincing – sheep refuges (unnecessarily high, and pointed), burial mounds (none in the world are this shape) – so you can construct your own explanation when you visit.

In *The Story of Sheppey* (2008), local man John Clancy has chronicled the loneliest place on this marginalised isle: Elmley. Out in the middle of the marshes, in Tudor times it recorded just six people taking communion in church. A century later, ten people took the host. Although in 1901 there were 319 residents and a pub, they all shopped by taking the three-penny ferry to the mainland, and this was Elmley's heyday. In 1919, when Kent County Council discovered that three of the five pupils in Elmley's school were children of the headmistress, they closed it down. Its ruins are visible near the RSPB office.

Elmley church had always been at odds with the authorities. In 1326, the local bishop condemned the inefficiency of the vicar. In later centuries, marriage and baptism records were not submitted annually, a legal requirement. In 1624, an Episcopal Visitation – a religious Ofsted inspection – simply called the church 'desolata'. During the eighteenth century, regular questionnaires – sent to all English churches – were ignored, except for the last one, which was sent back blank. Although visitors found cattle in the church and part of its roof missing in 1874, there are records of services there in 1934. By 1950, there had been no burials for nine years and the bishop issued a demolition order. Two years later, church officials found it still standing, although the local vicar, continuing the time-honoured local tradition of creative reporting, had written a while back to them to say that, yes, he had personally overseen the demolition. An investigation discovered that a Dover contractor had agreed to knock down the building. His bizarre excuse for not doing so was well within the Elmley tradition: he might have offended local landowners Oxford University by damaging the road with his trucks. But by 1954 the church was gone, ending over 600 years of bullshitting the authorities.

PUNISHED FOR TRYING TO HEAL HIS SHEEP

1363

The records of Kent's Church Courts are a fascinating window on medieval and Tudor life. These courts judged moral infringements, such as adultery, fornication and sodomy. Surprisingly, these sins of the flesh do not dominate the records: witchcraft and sorcery do. Until about 1600, the judges still believed in good and bad magic, white and black witches: their task was to distinguish between the two. As historian Karen Jones has found, all sorts of devilry was suspected, even 'sects of sexually promiscuous devil-worshippers'. Kent clearly had its dark, *Wicker Man* aspect.

Some of the less dramatic 'sins' are the strangest tales. Joanna Mores of Dover told the future by interpreting croaking frogs. Agnes Taylor of Westcliffe ended up in court for reporting the ghost of a neighbour's husband. Joan Squyer of Woodchurch, near Ashford, was found guilty of 'love-magic': she had stolen holy water and washed her husband's shirt with it! She believed he would thereby become 'obedient to her will'. As late as 1543, a Canterbury woman burned a candle over the 'dung of her enemy', a practice which was thought to make the enemy's bottom explode. The Church Courts wasted so much time on these absurdities that the records often read like an episode of *Blackadder*, but the punishments were far from amusing, and many women administering herbal remedies came under fire. The maddest case I learned of was that of Philip

Russell. In 1363, he was brought before the Rochester Diocesan Court for having put a toad in a bag around the neck of one of his sheep. It was an old folk remedy for curing ailing sheep, but Russell was publicly beaten in the marketplace as a punishment, a worse sentence than many fornicators received.

THE ALCHEMIST'S TOWER: VICTORIAN FOLLY OR MEDIEVAL SECRET?

c.1400

In the heart of old Canterbury, right on the river, stands the Alchemist's Tower. You can only touch the outside from a boat, but you can visit the inside by going to the far end of a rabbit-warren-like ancient shop in Best Lane. It's Multiyork Sofas at the moment. Although the tower was prettified by the Victorians, it stands on a Roman site and has medieval foundations. The tower is, in fact, a chimney and, inside, an old hearth is visible.

What was alchemy? It was the search for two things: the Philosopher's Stone, which could turn base metals into silver, and the search for the Panacea, which could cure all ills and give eternal life. This apparently ridiculous discipline reaches far back into Arabic, Egyptian, Chinese and Indian history. Although Pope John XXII, a Cahors cobbler's son, banned it by Edict in 1329, it was unstoppable. Nicholas Flamel (died 1418), whose house is the oldest in Paris, was said to have pulled it off, and found eternal life, hence his starring role in both *Harry Potter and the Philosopher's Stone* and *The Da Vinci Code*. Queen Elizabeth I's trusted astrologer John Dee devoted much of his life to the search for it, with her encouragement.

Potty though it appears, alchemy was the father of chemistry – Newton wrote more about alchemy than about physics – and, to Aquinas and Jung, it was a symbolic quest, an outward expression of all our searching for inner peace, a higher self. By the end of his life, Jung thought that all of his psychoanalytic theory was a mere continuation of the alchemical tradition. The survival of alchemy in the collective unconscious is demonstrated by the sales of Paulo Coelho's *The Alchemist*: 80 million copies. On a visit to Canterbury, Coelho told me that he originally wrote a gigantic history of alchemy, but, when his wife said it was boring, he distilled it – alchemy-style – into a short novel.

Anyone will tell you that Canterbury's Alchemist's Tower is a Victorian folly, built to attract tourists. But why go to all the trouble to build such an attraction in such an inaccessible place? You can only see it distantly from a bridge over the river. And there is something else: in 2011 I heard about the American family who visited Canterbury and asked to see Mitchell's Tower. Nobody could help them, until they said it was by the river, and their ancestor was Mitchell, a medieval alchemist.

Maybe our Alchemist's Tower is just a revamp of the real thing, and perhaps the Noble Art was practised in the very shadow of the cathedral.

THE WITCH QUEEN

1420

I cannot get her out of my head. I have just got up at two o'clock in the morning to write this tale because Joan of Navarre is so hypnotic. Of all the amazing women Kent has seen, Joan is one of the most intriguing and yet little-known. There is no biography. But I suppose that, if you were a woman in the Middle Ages, you were French, your father was called Charles the Bad, and you fell out with a national hero – Henry V of Agincourt fame – you could easily be forgotten.

Joan's roller-coaster life began in Normandy in 1368. Charles the Bad really was bad; utterly unprincipled and scheming. His death was a popular judgement fable: he was sewn into a brandy-soaked sheath – a bizarre health treatment – and a passing maid carrying a candle maid accidentally set him on fire. He went up like a Roman candle, fast-tracked to hell-fire. This happened when Joan was 20. At 18, she had been married off to the 47-year-old Duke of Brittany. By him, she dutifully produced eight children, before he died in 1399 at the age of 60.

Atypically for a dynastic union of the time, her next marriage, to King Henry IV of England, was a genuine love match. Joan had met Henry on diplomatic missions, and written warmly to him. When he proposed she accepted immediately and sailed for Dover. The ceremony was unusually intimate and authentic, held at the small west

Kent palace of Eltham, rather than in London. (Eltham was only officially absorbed by Greater London in 1899.) It was the first royal wedding to be conducted in English and the first use of the romantic formula 'thereto I plight thee my troth'. The couple loved Eltham and stayed there for an eight-week, working honeymoon. Henry built Joan a two-tier wing at Eltham Palace, with two large bay windows looking onto his 'Great Park', and gave her a magnificent £300 necklace; she had a lifelong love of fine clothing and jewellery. The King was a champion jouster – he started at 14 – a tough fighting monarch, but also a great lover of the arts. At Eltham he had a special two-tier desk made to accommodate his collection of books, at a time when Chaucer was regarded as exceptionally learned for having just 60 books.

The King gave Chaucer an annuity and encouraged poets to stay at his court. Joan and Henry were both passionate about music; his own compositions are still sold on CD. Henry and his Queen often visited Canterbury, for the innovative music scene there, because the archbishop was a close friend, and because the Becket cult resonated with the King. He installed a Becket stained-glass window in his Eltham study, above the aforementioned desk. And, though we might laugh at the idea now, at his coronation he was anointed with oil believed to have been given to Thomas Becket by the Virgin Mary herself. Guilt fuelled some of this royal devotion: Henry was excommunicated by the Pope for executing a rebellious Archbishop of York, although he was exculpated – the opposite of excommunication – after three years. In his will, Henry styled himself 'a sinful wretch.'

In 1400 Henry and Joan were visited by someone who sounds lie a character from One Thousand and One Nights: the 114th Emperor of the Byzantium, Manuel II. Following his journey from Constantinople, a colourful escort of English soldiers met him at Dover and escorted him to Canterbury, where he prayed at the Becket shrine. A monk commented on the long white robes and uncut beards of Manuel and his retinue. Manuel processed across Kent, roughly along the route of the M2, to spend Christmas at Eltham. He enjoyed 'a great mumming' or dramatic performance, and gave Henry a piece of Christ's tunic, another relic thought to have been woven by the Virgin Mary. Henry gave half of this cloth to be housed in a silver reliquary on the high altar at Canterbury Cathedral, next to some of Becket's blood and a section of the Crown of Thorns. (Poor old Manuel: while he was away Tamburlaine's Mongols sacked Aleppo, Damascus and Ankara.)

When Henry died, Joan commissioned the superb alabaster tomb you can see today – not at Westminster Abbey with England's other monarchs – but in Canterbury Cathedral. The wooden canopy is adorned with forget-me-knots and the entwined mottoes of the monarchs' two families. The face on the recumbent figure is an actual likeness. He has the outmoded hairstyle he affected, wears splendid robes and, as was noticed in 1995, jewellery that references the eagle-shaped, Virgin Mary oil casket used at his coronation. The tomb itself is as close as possible to Becket's, without invading that 'tomb-free zone', which reinforced the martyr's saintly status. Imagine the funeral: 45–year-old Joan tearful in her finery, superb choral music and – history records – an arrangement of candles that reached nearly to the roof-vault.

It had been a love-match, with no political advantage and little public support. Joan's arrival in England had been attended by rumours of fateful storms, and even a comet. Midway through her married years, Parliament demanded all Bretons be banished from England; Joan held onto her Breton servants only with difficulty. Henry had a complicated past. For dynastic reasons, he had married a 12-year-old ex-nun, Mary de Bohun, when he was 14. At 18, Mary gave birth to a boy who was to be his father's successor, Henry V, the hero of Agincourt.

Mary died in childbirth in 1394, before Joan's arrival in Henry IV's life. Joan had a lifelong talent for peace-making and was a good stepmother to Henry junior but, after Henry IV died, a strange volte-face occurred: Henry V turned against Joan. Crudely, he wanted her money for his war fund. First he confiscated many of her possessions. Then, in 1419, the 50-year-old Joan was accused by Father Randolph, her confessor, of using witchcraft to try and kill her stepson, the King. She was put under house arrest for three years, at Leeds Castle near Maidstone. Her liberty was restricted but she lived in tolerable comfort; Henry's main aim was accomplished – the confiscation of her estates. Just before his death he shamefacedly released her, and she enjoyed a peaceful final 15 years. She never did face a trial so the witchcraft accusation lingered in the popular imagination.

She is buried next to Henry in an adjoining alabaster tomb. Her effigy, with an impish face and petite stature, is hauntingly beautiful. Unlike Henry she is smiling, an inward, Mona Lisa smile. In 1832, the royal tomb was opened. Two elm-wood coffins lay side by side. Henry was found embalmed in still-moist leather wrappings, inside a sealed lead casket. When an opening was made over the face, it was intact, the skin tanned, the beard russet and matted. Within moments, the face crumbled to dust. Joan was left undisturbed in the darkness, far from her homeland but in the heart of Kent, where she found love and happiness.

THE WOMAN WHO WENT FROM HEAVEN TO HELL

1506–34

Elizabeth Barton was an illiterate Tudor servant-girl at Cobbs Hall, Aldington, near Ashford. At 19 years old, she stopped eating and, for several months, uttered prophecies and spiritual wisdom. In trance-like states, she recounted visions of heaven; she witnessed St Michael weighing souls in the balance, and she quoted Mary Magdalene. Understandably, the local priest rode to Canterbury to inform Archbishop William Warham, who met her, and was impressed. So was Thomas More, one of the finest minds of the Renaissance: he even asked Barton to pray for his family. She then had audiences with Cardinal Wolsey and Henry VIII himself. They both believed that she was divinely inspired. When the Papal Legate visited her, he kissed her feet.

In 1525, the Middle Ages were within living memory, and a visionary such as Barton was one of a long tradition of mystical women. Joan of Arc, Hildegard of Bingen, Julian of Norwich, St Brigid of Sweden and Catherine of Siena are the most famous. Every age comes to term with these puzzling figures in their own way.

To Freud and his followers they were classic cases of hysteria. In the 1980s, feminists defended them as misunderstood critics of the state. Since then, they have been identified, broadly, as schizophrenics with occasional anorexic tendencies and artistic talents.

Hildegard's music is still popular, and Julian of Norwich inspired T.S. Eliot.

Young Elizabeth came under celebrity pressure, being investigated by a special commission of monks. When she was inspired to visit the chapel of St Mary in Court-le-Street, near Aldington, 3,000 people gathered. One writer described her as England's Delphic Oracle.

Sadly, as with many celebrities, her fall was as steep as her ascent. When her prophecies opposed the King, official approval evaporated. Dangerously, she predicted that, should Henry divorce Katherine of Aragon and marry Anne Boleyn, he would not remain King for long. In the eyes of the Spanish ambassador and other Catholics, this prediction came true when the Pope excommunicated Henry, depriving him of divine kingship.

Elizabeth Barton had to be officially reassessed. She was interviewed by a radically Protestant new Archbishop, Thomas Cranmer, and by Henry's Machiavellian arch-fixer Thomas Cromwell, the man whose Durer portrait seems to fuse Uriah Heep and Jabba the Hutt. Elizabeth was sent to the Tower. After interrogation there, she was convicted of treason and sent to Canterbury, so that she could publicly confess to being a puppet of scheming Catholic monks. By now aged 28, she was then taken back to the Tower of London. From there, she was drawn on a cart to Tyburn, near today's Marble Arch, and hanged, then beheaded. Her head was displayed on London Bridge, so that the maximum number of passers-by could be reminded of the King's authority.

A 2004 study concluded that Elizabeth Barton was probably epileptic, an 'intelligent, courageous and charismatic woman'. Whether you believe this, or another historian who called her 'a liar and an exhibitionist', she was certainly a rare case of someone who saw heaven, and then was consigned to hell, within ten years in her short life.

THE PLANTAGENET BRICKLAYER

1550

Shakespeare was a great fan of the Tudor dynasty, so his plays celebrated its glorious beginning: the Battle of Bosworth in 1485. There the evil Richard III met his death, after uttering, in the play, the famous plea: 'A horse, a horse, my kingdom for a horse!' In film and on stage, Laurence Olivier and Anthony Sher have immortalised the hunchbacked monster.

With Richard III's death, the reign of the Plantagenets came to an end. 'Plantagenet' comes from the Latin name of broom: one of the King's ancestors wore a sprig in his hat. The dynasty included the Crusader, Richard the Lionheart, the signer of Magna Carta, King John, Chaucer's patron, Richard II, the founder of the jury system, Henry II, and the victor of Agincourt, Henry V. It was quite a family, with very strong personalities, mixing good and evil. As Richard the Lionheart once said, 'From the devil we come and to the devil we will go.' Henry II, Becket's nemesis, regularly outrode all his staff and had such a temper that he would writhe on the ground gnashing his teeth and roaring.

But did the dynasty really end at Bosworth? Fifty years after that battle, Thomas Moyle, a Speaker of the House of Commons under Henry VIII, was overseeing the building of his mansion at Eastwell Park, near Ashford. Moyle was intrigued by one of the bricklayers, a white-haired old man who took his breaks alone, reading a book. Literacy was unusual for a labouring man, so Moyle engaged him in conversation and heard his story. His name was Richard and he had been raised by a schoolmaster and well educated. A mysterious gentleman visited regularly to ensure that he was well and, one day, took him on a long horse-ride to a vast camp at Bosworth, buzzing with knights and bowmen. He was taken into a tent, where a stately man in rich armour told him, 'Richard, I am your father and if I win tomorrow I will provide for you as befits your blood. If I lose, I shall not see you again. I am King of England, but tell no one who you are unless I am victorious.' Richard the Plantagenet heir would, of course, be the first to be executed by the victorious Tudors. The King told Richard to watch the battle from a safe distance.

When the battle was lost, Richard fled to Kent, posing as a poor orphan. He told Moyle that his life had been happy, with reading as his great consolation. Moyle built him a cottage in Eastwell Park, which is still known as Plantagenet Cottage, and let him live out his retirement in reading and walking.

This is such an unlikely tale that by now the reader might well be dismissing it as nonsense, especially if he has checked the many books and internet sites on the Plantagenets, none of which mention this survivor.

And indeed for a long time the story seemed to be a fancy of Francis Peck, who told it in his rambling, rare, little-read, two-volume work of 1732, *Desiderata Curiosa, a collection of scarce and curious pieces relating to English History etc. etc....* (the title goes on for over 100 words).

But there is a stubborn fact. In Eastwell Parish Registers, there is this entry: 'Rychard Plantagenet was buryed on the 22 daye of December 1550'. Scholars have examined the entry; it is no forgery. The last descendant of Richard the Lionheart may well have been a retired bricklayer living near Ashford.

A PREGNANT CRAVING
FOR OYSTERS

1566

Thomas Harman was a Tudor squire with odd tastes who lived at Crayford, on a main road to London. Being laid up with a long-running illness, he started listening to the many beggars and vagabonds who called at the door of his house. He became adept at getting them to reveal the secrets of their trade, which he described in one of the first ever 'True Crime' books, *A Caveat for Common Cursitors*, published in 1566. The title means 'a warning for court officers'. It was no moral tract, and Harman grew to like his rogues and villains, lovingly recording their unique lingo in the first glossary of criminal slang. The book was a huge bestseller, and fed Shakespeare's interest in low-life characters, with all their vigour and lack of airs and graces. As this tale shows, they were natural storytellers.

A comely female beggar told Harman about her irresistible craving for oysters while she was pregnant. She 'lusted marvellously' after them and journeyed to Whitstable, where she opened and ate them where she found them. 'At last,' she went on, 'in seeking more, I reached after one, and stepped into a hole and fell in, into the waist, and there did stick.' She shouted loudly to a distant figure, a local man who eventually heard and came running. The beggar quickly realised that her joy at being saved, combined with 'the great colour in her face' from struggling, had aroused the ardour of her rescuer. Although married, he refused to pull her from the mud unless she agreed to 'lie with him'. Seeing no alternative, this she agreed to do. He took her home and let her sleep in his barn.

Unfortunately for the would-be adulterer, the pregnant visitor told the wife of his intentions and, together, they plotted their revenge. At supper, the unsuspecting husband 'was very pleasant, and drank to his wife and munched apace'. Later that night, he pretended to go and check on his horse, in the barn. Once he had laid down and 'removed his hose', his victim uttered the code phrase, 'Fie for shame!' and five friends of the wife sprang out of hiding to give the errant husband a beating. After tying him up with his own hose they left him 'blustering, blowing, and foaming with pain and melancholy, saying that he would be revenged on them all'. But the assailants had all disguised their faces, and fled, taking the young beggar to safety in a nearby town.

WHAT SHAKESPEARE DID IN FAVERSHAM

c.1580

What? It seems improbable that Shakespeare worked and slept in Faversham, and wrote a play set there, but there is ample scholarly evidence for both assertions. There is no doubt about his working in Faversham: the drama group he toured with, 'The Lord Chamberlain's Men', played both Faversham and Dover. Shakespeare's travels were extensive and gave his plays much of their richness. He rarely made up his own plots, so he was always on the lookout for dramatic stories which illuminated the wilder shores of human nature. The earliest printed mention of Shakespeare was a satire against his magpie-like plot-stealing. A British historian, Raphael Holinshed (1529–80), inspired no fewer than a dozen of the bard's plays. Holinshed was a scholar, but a good populariser too. His *Chronicles of England, Scotland and Ireland* must have been one of Shakespeare's most-thumbed books. The witches in *Macbeth* come straight from the *Chronicles*. Holinshed revelled in the sensational details of Britain's strangest tales, whether of kings or commoners.

Holinshed devoted a long passage to a real-life Faversham murder. Alice Arden felt neglected by her workaholic husband Tom, a busy entrepreneur and ex-Mayor of Faversham. She fell in love with Mosby, the brother of her maid, and, using his grubby connections with Faversham's underclass, she arranged for two thugs to murder Tom.

This was done one winter's evening in 1553, at 7.30p.m., in the parlour of his own house. The house and its garden remain intact to this day, a measure of the murder's dark fascination. Holinshed is the main source for the full horror of the affair: the thugs were incompetent, and it took several attempts before they succeeded in killing Arden. They dumped his body in the countryside near Faversham, hoping for the heavy snowfall to hide their footprints. It started thawing, and conclusively showed up their tracks. Alice was convicted and burned at the stake. Mosby and one of the thugs were hanged. The other escaped by boat down Faversham Creek and probably to Calais, with which he had connections.

The anonymous Tudor play, *Arden of Feversham*, has an unprecedented subtlety. Alice is no simple villain, but a tortured figure. She rues falling for Mosby, even as she pursues the murder plot. And Mosby wonders how he can ever trust a woman who can so betray her husband, musing, 'How can I sleep with a serpent?' As in *Macbeth*, the slow slide into evil is hair-raisingly portrayed. Did Shakespeare write the play? Was he assisted by his friend, local man Christopher Marlowe? Shakespeare's output is as beset with wacky theories as the Pyramids. I will merely summarise, therefore, the seven hard facts which support his authorship, or part-authorship, of *Arden of Feversham*. You can then decide, and your guess is as good as any scholar's, indeed probably better, because they all have axes to grind, and nests to feather:

1. Holinshed. As mentioned above, he gave much space to the murder, and he was the bard's single most-used source.

2. The quality of the play. One scholar avers that such subtlety only arrived in British drama with Shakespeare. Even the judicious poet T.S. Eliot

thought it must be by someone notable, although he suggested Shakespeare's contemporary Thomas Kyd. Other poets, notably Algernon Swinburne, saw Shakespeare's hand in it.

3. Computer analysis. In 2006, Newcastle University and the Institute of Renaissance Studies concluded that large sections of the play were by Shakespeare, reflecting his verbal patterns and tone. Typically: 'Black night hath hid the pleasures of the day, and sheeted darkness covers the earth'.

4. It is known that Shakespeare stayed in Faversham for a while.

5. Shakespeare's acting company, whose repertoire mostly comprised his own plays, staged *Arden of Feversham*.

6. The two murderers speak with un-thuggish sophistication. Did Shakespeare play one of them? In the play – but not in real life – they are called Black*will* and *Shak*bag (my italics). Such punning was common in Tudor writing.

7. Who published *Arden of Feversham*? Edward White, who also published Shakespeare plays.

One day, as strange as it may sound, Faversham may conclusively join Venice and Verona as the scene of one of Shakespeare's great love tragedies.

'A NEW EPOCH IN THE HUMAN MIND'

1584

Just north of the Hythe–Ashford road is the parish of Smeeth. In 1799 it had 'a rough and lonely appearance, with little traffic'. You can still see some rhythmic undulations in one of the fields. They are the ghostly reminder of an extraordinary man and a remarkable house. Wherever you are sitting reading this, imagine you see, like a large, old jigsaw with parts in darkness, the interior of an ancient mansion. It is morning, but the fire roars, for outside the landscape is flat and frozen. Samuel Pepys enters. He is visiting his old friend, Sir Thomas Scott. Unbelievably, Pepys' entire journey from London has been on Scott's land. The house is Scot's Hall, the centre of a huge estate since late medieval times, and this tale is about Scott's Tudor ancestor Reginald Scott.

Reginald Scott quietly revolutionised our world view in the manner of that later Kent resident, Charles Darwin. Unpropitiously, he dropped out of Oxford University without a degree, went home to Scot's Hall and immersed himself in gardening and, a contemporary wrote, 'solitary reading'. At the age of 30, in 1568, he married a local girl, Jane Cobbe, whose family home in Aldington still stands, with walls 2ft (61cm) thick. By the time he was 36, the gardening had led to a treatise on hop-farming, a book that formed the foundation stone of Kent's hop industry, and which was written with the stated intention to help poor yeomen prosper. The printer inserted an irritated note admitting to textual errors owing to Scott's home-loving refusal to visit London to oversee the printing process.

When he was 46, his *Discovery of Witchcraft* (1584) was published. This 500-page manual of witchcraft and magic drew on hundreds of old texts and on the proceedings of witch trials. Its depth of learning, from a university drop-out immured on the edge of Romney Marsh, still puzzles historians. Outwardly, it was an occult encyclopaedia, ground-breaking in its detail: Shakespeare used it for his *Macbeth* witches and his *Midsummer Night's Dream* fairies, and it is still a *vade mecum* in magic circles.

But look more closely: Scott dedicated the book to help those 'at the frontiers of povertie', especially women, children, and vulnerable country folk. The book, with its vein of acid sarcasm and ridicule of absurd rites, forensically debunked belief in witchcraft and showed up witch-burning – then at its height – as barbaric. Elizabeth Barton, a servant-girl in the house of Scott's own wife, had been executed for witchcraft even though Thomas More believed that her visions were divinely inspired. Not only were there no witches in England, Scott averred, but all those burned were innocent. Furthermore, all supposed mentions of 'witch' in the Bible were mistranslations. He did defend herbal medicine, however, and showed a very Freudian awareness that some diabolic experiences seemed very real to the experiencer.

Scott was playing with fire in every sense, and his book was a Europe-wide sensation – he could have faced execution himself. The printer was protected by being named only at the end of the book, with no address. Jean Bodin, the respected French philosopher and law professor, called Scott 'an accomplice of the Devil'. King James called Scott 'that damnable heretic', ordered every copy of the book to be burned (ensuring – such is human nature – wide circulation) and personally wrote the book *Demonology*, a counterblast to Scott that reeked of hellfire and damnation.

Scott lived on peacefully at Scot's Hall, dying there aged 61. How did he get away with it?

Partly, it was the perennial Scott family mystique that so charmed Pepys. Henry VI trusted a Scott to be Lieutenant of the Tower of London. Edward IV employed a Scott as Controller of the Royal Household and gave him not only the estates of Chilham Castle, but also all the lands of the Bishop of Durham and Earl of Oxford, who had fallen out of favour. Richard III had a Scott adviser, under Henry VII one was MP for Kent and Governor of Calais, and Henry VIII knighted another. When someone asked Elizabeth I about ennobling a Scott she said, 'No, sir – they've already got more power in Kent than I have.' A kinsman of Reginald Scott told Elizabeth to her face that she had 'no more control over her passions than an untamed heifer'.

More personally, Scott was a member of the Family of Love, a Europe-wide Christian sect, which denied the very existence of the devil. The Family's founder, German mystic Henry Nicholis, had visions and heavenly directions from boyhood onwards. Flung into jail as a madman by the Germans, he fled to more relaxed Amsterdam and visited England, spreading his quietist message. Followers included the printer Christopher Plantin, and the painter Breughel the Elder. Queen Elizabeth's lack of action when told that most beefeaters were Familists has led some to think she sympathised, or was even a member. The Family's ideas were so radical that it operated largely in secret – even today academics do not fully understand it for this reason. *Scott's Discovery of Witchcraft* was inspired in both its message and its coded methodology by Familist ideals.

Scott's Familism fuelled his books and also the philanthropy behind 'the greatest feat of Tudor engineering' – the building of Dover Harbour, complete with sluices to keep it silt-free. The harbour saved countless lives, and was the work of Scott and Kentish mathematician Dudley Digges.

Scott's detailed instructions for the labourers' decent pay and conditions survive. He had Romney Marsh protected from flooding as well. Again, scholars marvel at how he acquired engineering skills in his bucolic retreat.

He wrote his own will, charmingly: 'to my grand-daughter Cicely £10 to buy a little Chaine ... £6 to my daughter-in-law Marie to be spent on Apparel but not to let her mother take any of the money ... and the rest to my wife for great is the trouble she has had with me and small is the comfort she has received at my hands'.

Looking back from Victorian times, Disraeli's father marvelled that 'from the privacy of a retired student can come a single book which marks a new epoch in the human mind'. Scott lies in lonely Smeeth church, where the roof leaks, but he has more merit than many a dignitary in Westminster Abbey.

THE LONG QUEST TO BE POSH

1598–1644

The life of Edward Dering of Pluckley, near Ashford, was one long quest to be truly posh. He was born inside the Tower of London, where his father was Lieutenant, but he rapidly became lord of the manor at Pluckley. Queen Elizabeth's minister Lord Burghley famously said, 'Nobility is nothing but ancient riches.' Lacking the riches, Dering tried other tactics.

He moved fast. By the age of 21, things were looking up: he had married Anne, Lady Ashburnham, and was mercilessly using her connections to the Earl of Buckingham to get noticed at Court. Via that connection, he became a baronet at 29.

When, in the same year, his wife died young and Buckingham was assassinated, Dering was, socially, out in the cold again.

His next opportunity was Mrs Bennett, a rich widow, but, although Edward spent heavily on bribing her servants to further his cause, she married someone else. His unpublished diary of the Mrs Bennett campaign is a Pooteresque masterpiece.

Two further marriages did little to raise Dering's position, so he followed his father's course of becoming lieutenant of a royal property – Dover Castle – but even this proved a financial failure, as Dering had to pay a handsome sum to his predecessor to secure the poorly paid post.

He kept a meticulous notebook recording his expenditure, and it fascinatingly records his struggles for status. (I am grateful to retired archivist Laetitia Yeandle, who recently transcribed all 400 pages.) As a young man, he dined at a tavern with three Kentish Lords, all of whom proclaimed ancient ancestry. 'My people go back to the Saxons' has been the perennial boast of English aristocrats ever since the rise of the *nouveau riche* gentry in Tudor times.

Dering did not have such ancestry, so he simply made it up. A keen heraldry researcher, he purchased a genuine, gigantic, medieval illuminated manuscript, 9ft (2.7m) long, listing all 300 noble ancient families in England. Made in Dover and now called the Dering Roll, the British Library bought it in 2008 for £200,000. After the purchase, British Library experts discovered that Dering had carefully erased one of the families, inserting a fictitious 'Sir Edward Fitz-Dering' complete with a fine, invented, coat of arms.

In 1624, Dering paid for this crest to be carved in brass and mounted in the hall at his Pluckley manor. In 1625, he bought eight suits of clothing for his servants, embroidered with the crest. In 1626, he had old-looking stained-glass versions of the crest put in his 'inner study' and parlour windows. In 1627, he recorded paying for his arms to be stamped onto the outside of his leather books, the crest supported by a wyvern, the dragon of the Saxons. Then, finding an ancient sword locally, he paid for it to be stripped of rust, repaired and emblazoned with the crest. Another expense was the purchase of reams of 'Italian Royal Paper', embossed with the 'Dering Arms'.

You've just got to admire the *chutzpah* of Sir Edward's final stroke of genius. He inserted several fake ancient Dering monuments in Pluckley church, to provide lasting evidence of his breeding.

Like so many likeable fantasists, Sir Edward brightened up our world and was, for all his eccentricity, a force for good. A Renaissance man, he donated large sums to the poor, and tipped handsomely wherever he went. He gambled at cards frequently, but always seemed to lose. He loved dressing up and going to plays. Centuries after his death, the earliest-known version of any Shakespeare play was found among Dering's papers at his Pluckley manor. He is like one of Shakespeare's lovable, pompous characters and I like to think that the two may have met.

WHERE THE USA BEGAN
1620

Many Canterbury passers-by must wonder about the battered old painting on the front of 59 Palace Street. I know I did for many years. High up above the shopfront, it depicts, in the romantic style of an old biscuit-tin picture, a sailing ship on the high seas.

I have noticed Americans often photographing this little building. Small wonder – for as strange as this might sound – this is where the USA began. It is typical of Kent, with its onion-layers of history everywhere, that there is no plaque on Number 59.

Robert Cushman was a Canterbury Puritan of such strong dissenting beliefs that he was imprisoned in the city's Westgate Towers prison. The reaction of Cushman and his Puritan friends was extreme: they would sell their homes in order to found a free-speech colony in America, a little-known wilderness that Columbus had discovered just 128 years before. At 59 Palace Street, Robert Cushman signed the agreement to lease the *Mayflower* – the ship in the old painting – in which his Puritan colleagues were to emigrate to America. One of the so-called 'Pilgrim Fathers' of America, Cushman himself sailed out on a different ship, landing in Plymouth, Massachusetts, to face a bleak midwinter. Many friends had died on the voyage out. Gathering the few colonists together, Cushman made a rousing speech on 9 December, exciting members of the pioneer nation to put their own needs second to the colony's survival. He set the tone for centuries of future Presidential speeches, such as J.F. Kennedy's 'Ask not what your country can do for you, but what you can do for your country'. The Massachusetts community survived, and federated with later settlements into the Thirteen Colonies, the nucleus of the United States of America. If Canterbury's authorities had not thrown Cushman into a dungeon, American history could have been very different.

THE MOST HATED MAN IN KENT HISTORY?

1662

Richard Culmer, vicar, was like a *Blackadder* character. A strict Puritan, his lifelong campaign to impose his views on others is comical in its extremism. Born near Broadstairs in about 1597, Culmer started 'kicking off' as a Puritan when he was Vicar of Goodnestone, near Wingham, east of Canterbury. There, his refusal to use less-than-Puritan prayer books was reported to the Archbishop by his congregation and he was suspended from office. Undeterred, he got a job as assistant to the vicar of Harbledown (just west of Canterbury), and campaigned against the villagers playing sport on Sunday. He used his children as spies to report this infringement: the sportsmen stoned the poor kids.

Fired up by the outbreak of the English Civil War, he entered Canterbury Cathedral to destroy 'all monuments of superstition'. By now a prolific Puritan writer, he later gloated in print about how he had stood on a 60-step ladder with a pikestaff, smashing stained-glass windows. It says much for the people of Canterbury that they turned out *en masse* to stop Culmer, or 'Blue Dick', as he had become known (he wore blue robes). Culmer's account omits to mention that, as the townspeople approached, he weed himself in the cathedral, for fear, his son said, that they would 'knock out his brains'. Like many bullies, he seems to have been a coward at heart. The new Puritan government allowed him to become a full vicar again, but he was so disliked by his new flock at Chartham that he moved on to Minster, near Ramsgate. He soon made his mark there by refusing to preach on Christmas Day. For this, his parishioners assaulted him in the churchyard, calling him a rogue. Locals used to make merry around the maypole at Minster. An intoxicating, whirling process, it was the ancient version of a rave, associated with all sorts of loucheness, very different from its 'hey nonny-no' image. (To this day, London's Mayfair, once the site of a huge pole, is openly a prostitutes' quarter because of this association.) When Culmer raged against such paganism, a reveller told him that, nearby, 'there was a bough strong enough to hang him on'. Soon afterwards, Culmer sued several locals to get unpaid church rents out of them. A collection was raised to plead with Parliament to remove Blue Dick; the villagers donated an extraordinary £300 to this worthy cause, but to no avail.

Desperate, they locked him out of the church for two weeks. He climbed in through a broken window. Determined, they removed the bell-clapper, so that he could not summon them to services. He replaced it with his wife's iron pestle from the kitchen. At their wits' end, they pulled him from the pulpit in mid-rant, and crushed him with a plank until he vomited blood. Still he would not go. He popped into Canterbury for a day. They had not forgotten him there; mud was thrown at him and some enthusiastic locals tried to hang him.

Three pamphlets were published against Culmer, one simply entitled *Antidotum Culmerianum* (An Antidote to Culmer). In the end, only the Restoration of the Royalists stopped Culmer's career, and he was forcibly retired. He lived out his remaining days in Monkton, Thanet, before dying in 1662. From the grave, he hassled his poor flock, whining in his will: 'many sums of money are due to me from occupiers of lands'. Even 50 years after his death,

John Lewis, the then Vicar at Minster, would write: 'no man was ever more hated ... and is to this day spoken of with all dislike imaginable'.

Did he have a soft side? It is hard to find; he had seven children, all forged into little Puritans. His son wrote an admiring memoir (source for the incontinence moment), insisting that he had a sense of humour, but citing very unfunny examples of it. The strange tale of Culmer has one advantage: it demonstrates the extraordinary vigour of Kent's resistance to Puritanism.

A MEDICI, A MASSACRE
AND A DOORWAY
TO THE PAST

1685

Canterbury has a time-travel portal, a low door on the outside of the cathedral, always apparently locked, with a faded sign in French next to it. Each Sunday at 3p.m. it is unlocked, and a French pastor conducts a service, in French, for a small, ageing congregation. This obscure, little-known ritual is part of an ancient struggle which made the Europe we live in.

In 1536, a lawyer's son from Picardy in northern France published a sharp critique of Christianity. He was John Calvin and his theories became known as Calvinism: a belief that the individual could deal directly with God, through following the Bible. Corrupt bishops, and even the Pope, Calvin said, simply got in the way of individual communication with God. The Bible, and church services, should be in English. Transubstantiation, the idea that the host turned into Christ's body by a miracle during the mass, was nonsense. Eventually, Calvin's ideas would merge with Luther's into Protestantism and take over England. Canterbury has been called England's 'Calvinist hub', a fortress in the great war of ideas that was the Reformation. Although France remained Catholic, by 1570, about 2 million of its 16 million inhabitants followed Calvinism. These were the Huguenots, and Canterbury, along with Spitalfields in London, became their safe haven from persecution. Henry VIII's son King Edward VI, who abolished, in England, both the mass and the celibacy of priests, was so sympathetic to Huguenots that he gave them the crypt at Canterbury to worship in, in French.

In France, there followed over 150 years of sustained persecution. In 1572, Paris witnessed the massacre of over 10,000 Protestants under Charles IX. The King's scheming Catholic mother Catherine De Medici inspired this, the St Bartholomew's Day Massacre, although Charles IX's screaming 'Kill them all, Kill them all!' shows that he was no slacker. In 1593, the French King Henry IV, a desultory Protestant, realised that his future popularity and security lay in going back to the Papal mainstream. With the immortal phrase 'Paris is worth a mass', he converted to Catholicism.

Anti-Huguenot persecution intensified over the coming years. In 1685, the Sun King, Louis XIV, issued the Edict of Fontainebleau: all Huguenot churches and schools were to be closed down. Twenty thousand Huguenots fled to England, the largest immigration ever (in percentage terms). Many stayed in Kent, mostly at Canterbury. France's loss was an English gain. Huguenots were highly literate. One study found that they owned roughly double the amount of books that a Catholic family owned. And they were highly skilled, especially in silk-making and weaving, paper-making and horticulture (they brought celery to England). Canterbury's much-photographed Weavers' Houses only stopped resounding to the clack of looms in 1914, and soon after the Edict of Fontainebleau there were over 900 looms in Canterbury. Weavers needed a lot of light and in a backstreet, Turnagain Lane, an ancient top storey is still lit by a long 'weavers' window'.

The Huguenot churches of Faversham, Sandwich and Maidstone closed long ago, but, in a small chapel of Canterbury Cathedral crypt, the Huguenots have continued their services to this day. Their little separate exterior doorway is indeed a portal to the past. The faded wooden sign reads *'Église Protestant Francaise'*.

A ONE-MAN
ENLIGHTENMENT

1749

Christopher Marlowe is Kent's Renaissance Man, but Kent's Enlightenment Man is unknown and elusive. He was Christopher Packe, a hero of science whose epic struggles against ignorance typify the Enlightenment, that great movement towards Reason which is usually identified with Edinburgh and London. Packe (1686–1749), a humble Canterbury doctor for decades, was lucky in his ancestry. His father, also Christopher Packe, was a professor of chemical medicine whose laboratory was located at the Pullman-esque 'Sign of the Globe and Chemical Furnaces', in London's Moorfields. He published several texts on pharmacy. His grandfather, also Christopher Packe, resisted the despotism of Charles I and supported Cromwell, who made him Mayor of London and recognised the trademark Packe all-round ability by appointing him to 71 committees. (Let's draw a veil over his corruption and anti-Semitism, which were then commonplace.)

So Christopher Packe, the Canterbury doctor, came from a long line of men on the side of Reason and Progress. Unsurprisingly, he found his long horseback rides to the sick of Canterbury district tedious, until he began to use the trips to think about maps. As early as 1737, decades before the Ordnance Survey, he made a map of the Canterbury area. One of the reasons he remains unknown is the apparently mad way he presented this pioneer map.

He called it 'Philosophical Cartography', and noted that rivers irrigated the land in exactly the same way that the arteries and veins 'irrigated' the body with oxygen. Blood circulation was still an exciting new idea, first expounded in 1628. Packe studied the Stour and its many little tributaries, and worked out why it ran where it did, discovering its twin sources with excitement. He wrote: 'The valleys and their waters differ but little from the arteries, veins and nerves that are with such exquisite art distributed all through our bodies.' On reflection, this is less a mad idea, and more of a presentiment of James Lovelock's ground-breaking twentieth-century Gaia theory of life on earth: Packe is an unsung eco-pioneer.

When he journeyed to London to present his ideas to the Royal Society, they were well received, and Packe began a long correspondence with a Royal Society member, Hans Sloane, the founder of the British Museum. Encouraged, Packe resolved to make a second, better map. To get a good vantage point, he erected a large wooden scaffolding on top of Canterbury Cathedral's 235ft (71.6m) Bell Harry tower. The doctor in frock coat and wig, holding his huge wood-and-brass theodolite on such a perilous structure, is surely one of the Enlightenment's heroic images. It is comparable with Benjamin Franklin flying kites in storms to investigate lightning.

Packe's passion for Reason was on display in his medical practice too. One of his patients was Robert Worger, concussed from falling off his horse. Worger's family, frustrated with his rate of recovery, deserted Packe and took Robert to good old Dr John Gray, an ill-educated Canterbury doctor who still believed in 'trepanning'. This medical practice goes back to prehistoric times and involves drilling a hole in the patient's skull to 'release pressure'. Soon after his ordeal, Worger died. It was just the sort of superstitious practice, like witch-burning, which the Enlightenment specialised in terminating. Packe published a vigorous demolition of Gray's medical practices, which was widely circulated and hastened the end of trepanation.

Dr Packe died in peaceful obscurity. The church where he was buried, in Canterbury's Burgate, was demolished in 1871. His tomb is no more. I hope this strange tale sheds fresh light on this likeable Kent polymath.

KENT'S WOODEN MASTERPIECE SAVED BY TEARS

1759

Chatham Dockyard is a World Heritage Site with good reason; it is a unique pre-industrial factory. For most of its working life (from Tudor times onwards), it emitted no pollution and made ships powered by wind and currents alone, from sustainable Kent woodland. Sailors of the time were so aware of sustainability that one admiral, on his daily walk, used to scatter acorns from his pockets in fertile spots, to provide future oak for ships.

At Chatham, these ships were built with an intricate knowledge of how wood and hemp-rope can be crafted to last. So 400ft (122m) long rope-walk sheds can still be seen, home of the fine art of twisting rope, thicknesses varying from ½in (1.3cm) to that of a man's arm. In man-made lakes known as 'Mast Ponds', tree-length logs floated until they were seasoned enough to withstand any weather. Incredibly, these spars were joined with wooden dowels rather than rust-prone nails.

It is now recognised that these great ships were the largest man-made structures of their day apart from cathedrals, built to withstand conditions from arctic to tropical. Yet, surprisingly, Chatham's master shipwrights are unknown and uncredited. After much ferreting about in the small print of specialist ship literature, I discovered that Kent native John Lock was the shipwright who built HMS *Victory* in 1759, to plans by naval architect Sir John Slade. This was, of course, the ship on which Lord Nelson died in a much-painted scene. His deathbed phrase, 'Kiss me, Hardy', is as famous as the signal he flew, 'England expects that every man will do his duty'.

How this ship lasted! It was made from seventeenth-century trees. Shakespeare toured Kent with his acting company and – let's be whimsical – could easily have seen one of them as a young oak. Lock would have literally walked the woods of the Weald to select mature oaks for the various parts of the *Victory*, the search for the massive Y-shaped keelson being the most crucial. The Battle of Trafalgar was in 1805, when the *Victory* was already 46 years old, a veteran of three other sea battles.

There was no heritage mentality about these 'cathedrals of the sea'. One ship, another veteran of Trafalgar, was destroyed as late as 1947. It was so well built, however, as to be almost unsinkable. Painful to relate, it was torched, holed and finally bombed from the air before it slowly sank in front of a small audience of visibly moved sailors. Even the historic *Victory* was ordered to be broken up, ironically by Thomas 'kiss me' Hardy himself, within 20 years of Trafalgar. When Hardy, by then First Sea Lord, came home and informed his wife, she allegedly burst into tears and sent him straight back to the office to reverse the order.

So Kent's wooden masterpiece, HMS *Victory*, made of Kentish oak, is now preserved and on display in Portsmouth (it seems, thanks to Mrs Hardy's emotional outburst). It is the world's oldest naval ship, and has even survived a Luftwaffe bomb. The ship's topsail, also made at Chatham, pierced by 90 cannonballs, is on display nearby.

EGERTON BRYDGES:
SCOUNDREL OR SCHOLAR?

1762–1837

Born into wealth, Brydges attended the King's School, Canterbury. He seemed to fritter away both his wealth, and his reputation. After legal training, he was called to the Bar but could never be bothered to practise. Instead he moved to Denton Court, near Dover, and blew a fortune on lavishly refurbishing it. Although he once wrote that he had 'married much too early', he mercilessly exploited his wife's aristocratic lineage, claiming that, as a result of his marriage, he, not George III, should be king. Determined to be noble in his own right, he claimed to be the thirteenth Baron Chandos. He tried to prove the claim in a case heard at the House of Lords, by peers. The affair dragged on for 12 years, ending in the humiliation of Brydges: he was descended from humble yeomen of Harbledown, a village near Canterbury. In trying to prove his outrageous claim, Brydges had falsified entries in parish registers.

Now Brydges gets even more interesting. Most men would be broken by such a public rebuff, but Brydges not only continued to style himself Baron Chandos, he also added the letters 'S.J.' to his name. This stood for the Swedish Order of the Knights of St Joachim, and entitled Egerton to be called '*Sir* Egerton Brydges'. The Order was totally bogus. His next four moves were even more scandalous. Although he remained at Denton Court, he bought Sudely Castle, a mansion in Gloucestershire, the ancestral home of the first, medieval, Baron Chandos. Then he personally edited a nine-volume edition of *Peerage of England*, mainly to show that his claim to be Baron Chandos was valid. He followed this up with a dense legal treatise which showed that peers had no legal right over other peers, thus invalidating the Lords' judgement against him.

When Brydges' money finally ran out, he fled to Europe and wrote his hilariously self-advertising memoirs. He was down, but not out. In 1826, he returned to Kent and tried to recover his fortune, it appears, by a complicated fraud. It failed. His sons were co-conspirators: one fled to die in poverty in France and the other, the vicar of Denton, was jailed. The dilapidated Denton Court was demolished.

Finally, in 1831, he published *Lex Terrae*. This was his right hook to the House of Lords: it proved that he was directly descended from Charlemagne, the Holy Roman Emperor.

Despite all this, a case can be made for Brydges. As an MP, he supported the Poor Law Act and championed authors' copyright. He was plagued by a lifelong melancholy, so his recurrent schemes were probably manic-depressive episodes. His commitment to scholarship was lifelong; he was genuinely elected to the elite Society of Antiquaries, and he saved the ancient Gatehouse at Denton for posterity; it is now a listed building. Supremely, he was a publisher of old English literature, much of which might otherwise have been lost for ever. His own press at Lee Priory, Ickham, near Canterbury, churned out these works, including a much-praised edition of Milton which helped to bring that genius to a wider public. Poignantly, he always thought his finest work was his poetry, which flopped. His novel, satirising Kent provincial life, with its 'book-hating squires', fared better, and was read by Jane Austen, who knew Brydges and, it is often presumed, modelled Sir Walter in *Persuasion* on him. For all his vanity, Brydges had good intentions. He illustrates the old mystery: 'The saint and the sinner are merely exchanging notes.'

LOSING IT ALL,
GAINING IT ALL
1776–1839

Hester Stanhope lived at Chevening House, near Sevenoaks, until she was 24. Nobody growing up at Chevening could be quite normal: a 115-room Renaissance mansion with huge grounds, it was bequeathed to the nation when the Stanhope line died out, and is now the official residence of the Foreign Secretary. In 2011, Deputy Prime Minister Nick Clegg and Foreign Secretary William Hague began to enjoy regular swims in its lake. 'Very Brideshead', commented the *Guardian*, although my image of those particular individuals adrift is more 'very Famous Five'.

An independent and wilful child, Hester's response, aged four, to a telling-off from her grandmother was both touching and clever: 'Oh, Grandma, but for you I'd be good for nothing.' Hester's singularity was increased by the influence of her father, the 3rd Earl Stanhope. His gaunt, lanky figure featured regularly in Gillray cartoons, especially after he was the sole MP to support the new French Republic after the Revolution, earning him the nicknames 'Citizen Stanhope' and 'Minority of One'. At home, Stanhope pursued his passion for inventing, and pioneered the calculator and the use of electricity. As a parent, he was a distant tyrant. The brilliant Hester, who has generated five biographies, was not allowed access to books. 'My father,' she recalled, 'said reading destroys the mind and carefully locked up his 30,000 volumes,' presumably including his own book, *The Principles of Electricity*. Instead, she was set to minding turkeys on the local common. Nor was her physical self-esteem allowed to flourish. Whenever she procured an attractive dress, it was confiscated.

Her saviour was her mild-mannered, intellectual but fun uncle, William Pitt the Younger, who became Prime Minister in 1783. As Hester grew up, he took her to London, to parties and into society.

There her acid wit and disregard for convention made her popular and notorious. In 1803, during a three-year spell out of office, Pitt invited Hester to his Kent residence, Walmer Castle, to become the Lady of the Castle. While Pitt refurbished the rooms, Hester created a wild woodland garden amid the formal grounds. She called it The Glen, and it is still there, 200 years later. When Pitt regained the Premiership in 1804, Hester became the Lady of No. 10 Downing Street, entertaining brilliantly at glittering dinners. Uncle and niece were extremely close during these years. Her influence over Pitt as Prime Minister was always a matter of debate. When challenged, Pitt stonewalled: 'Hester and I have made a bargain. We each give each other advice on condition that neither takes it.'

Pitt's death, when Hester was 30, was a body blow. On his deathbed, he would sigh, 'Hester, where's my Hester?' Although Parliament voted Hester a huge pension – £1,200 a year – her material comfort was not matched by emotional support: she was to be disappointed in love. Earl Granville 'led her on' to believe he loved her, but it was all over suddenly when he took a job in Russia. Most of 'society' knew that he had all along been passionately involved with the much older Lady Bessborough. She then became close to General Moore and hoped for marriage, but he died in Spain, fighting the French. Soon afterwards, her beloved brother Charles died. Charles and Hester had woven a protected world together during their difficult Chevening childhood.

His death was too much to bear, after so much. She set sail for the East, away from the gossips of London. En route, in Greece, a fellow exile consoled her: Lord Byron swam out to greet her.

This final chapter of her life is her fame. She lived among the Bedouin, in Arab dress, becoming respected as the queen of her fortress mountain in Lebanon. Although travellers were shocked by her arabisation, and by the poplar poles propping up ceilings, she was on her own mystical journey. She wrote of reuniting with nature, and diagnosed Western civilisation as sick from lack of closeness to it. As she evolved her own personal religion, drawing on Islam, older Syrian creeds, doctrines of reincarnation and Christianity, she was called a madwoman by most Westerners.

Parliament stopped her pension. But local Arabs thought she had the gift of divination. She spent eight days with a mountain hermit, who taught her Sufism (mystical Islam). Such was her position in the Arab world that, when Egypt was about to invade Lebanon, they first asked for her neutrality. She accepted fewer and fewer visitors, but one little-known late account by a female visitor is interesting: 'I am quite sure that, whatever may be the eccentricity of Lady Hester Stanhope, her mind is unimpaired, and that few women can boast of more real genius and active benevolence.' Near the end, Hester wrote with delight: 'My fortune's melted away, I require no luxuries. The older I grow the less, thank God, I need, and the more eagerly I draw near to nature.'

What a journey: from tending turkeys in Kent to Eastern mystic on a Lebanese mountain, via Walmer Castle and Number 10. Perhaps the emotional odyssey was greater: from strictly disciplined childhood at Chevening, to a desperately close love of her uncle, then the desolation of a broken heart and her brother's death, to a sort of peace.

UNDER THIS OAK, SLAVERY WAS SLAIN

1787

Why did an anti-slavery society recently pay for the restoration of an oak tree in Kent? I had never realised how dark slavery was until I researched this tale. Every schoolboy learns about the three-month journeys in battery-chicken conditions from Africa to the Americas, with deaths on the way. But I was shocked into stillness by the statistic from 1775, a year when 75,000 black people were shipped from their homes in Africa, across the Atlantic to America. And it is almost unbearable to read about the Liverpool-owned *Zong*. The captured black people on this ship were dying so rapidly from poor conditions that the Captain, Englishman Luke Collingwood, realised he would get little money for his 'cargo' on arrival in Jamaica. But in those days – 1781, with Europe listening to Mozart – Collingwood could get £30 a head from his insurance company for 'lost cargo'. He pushed 122 people into the sea, the later ones in chains, because they knew their fate and had started to struggle. His first mate opposed the massacre, triggering a famous London trial at which the defence asserted: 'Blacks are goods'.

William Wilberforce began the political anti-slavery movement on a spring 1787 visit to Prime Minister Pitt the Younger's mansion at Holwood, near Bromley. They were old friends, and Pitt loved 'cutting and planting' in Holwood's grounds. For Kentish-born Pitt, Holwood was a necessary retreat from politics and from his port-addicted London lifestyle. The two men went for a walk in the grounds, a walk that would change history. Wilberforce wrote years later: 'I well remember, after a conversation with Mr Pitt in the open air at the foot of an old tree at Holwood, just above the steep descent into the vale of Keston, I resolved to bring about the abolition of slavery.' Soon afterwards his anti-slavery movement achieved the setting up of a House of Commons inquiry into slavery, during which the secretive Customs Office opened its records on the money they got from the practice. When slavers protested that abolition would merely give the business to France and Spain, Pitt pressured those two governments to consider abolition. When Wilberforce was bed-bound with ulcerative colitis before his big parliamentary anti-slavery speech, Prime Minister Pitt, out of friendship and in memory of their oak-tree conversation, agreed to make the speech himself. When Wilberforce recovered, he followed up with a speech which wowed the legendary orator Edmund Burke. 'That was better than Demosthenes himself!' he exclaimed.

But abolition was to be a long haul. Pitt died of drink and exhaustion in 1806. Britain banned the slave trade throughout their empire in 1807, but not the holding of slaves. In Wilberforce's last year, when he was a frail 74-year-old in 1833, he made his last anti-slavery speech, back in Kent at a public meeting in Maidstone. He must have recalled sitting on the grass under that oak tree with his much-loved friend Pitt 46 years earlier. A few months after his Maidstone speech, on the day before he died, he was told about the successful passage of the Slavery Abolition Bill. The taxpayer gave the slave-traders an eye-watering £20 million in compensation. Wilberforce was buried in Westminster Abbey next to Pitt.

What about the oak tree? Much revered as the 'Tree of Liberty', it survived the 1987 hurricane but blew down in a 1991 gale. American anti-slavery campaigners planted a new oak at the site. And, satisfyingly, the oak's spirit may live on: a Victorian politician sent acorns from it to a Canadian lawyer, Henry Crease. Crease's mansion is long gone but his garden remains and there, in Victoria, British Columbia, are two fine healthy old oak trees.

THE SECRET HISTORY OF THE CHANNEL TUNNEL

1802–2001

It is one of the wonders of the world. Recently, a panel of architects named the Channel Tunnel 'the construction project of the twentieth century'. As an achievement, they decided that it beats such wonders as the Golden Gate Bridge and the Sydney Opera House. To lose £900 million in one year – 1995 – and go on to make a profit by 2000, is also something of a wonder. But this tunnel we now take for granted has a little-known heritage that is a strange tale indeed.

To even join the two countries seems like a mad ambition, and a madman – Caligula – was indeed the first to explore the idea. He proposed a bridge made up of ships lashed to each other, and even made a 2 mile (3.2km) prototype off Italy before his death. A candlelit Channel Tunnel for carriages was designed in 1802. Then, in 1851, a tunnel which would gracefully sink to the seabed gained favour. With its glass roof, and Gothic ventilation turrets in the Channel, it foundered because of cost – £87 million – despite backing from the monarchy: Queen Victoria suffered badly from seasickness. A Dr Laconne had a cheaper proposal, a mind-boggling idea: a seabed railway *without a tunnel*. By 1985, several options were being seriously considered, including a bridge held up by airships, and the 'Expressway': a tunnel in which cars drove over submerged railway tracks which were used, every now and then, by trains.

In 1986, the Treaty of Canterbury – signed at the cathedral's Chapter House – ended the debate and committed the two governments to the tunnel as now constructed. Invasion fears led to secret schemes to disable the tunnel. Cunning British generals wanted a small nuclear bomb fitted into the tunnel for this purpose. They only abandoned this plan when MoD boffins pointed out that, as well as disabling the tunnel, it would turn it into a double-ended nuclear cannon and devastate Kent and northern France. Tunnel security is still covered by the Official Secrets Act but the long-established in-house journal of SNCF, *La Vie Du Rail*, alleges that there is a secret panic button at either end to flood the tunnel, if either London or Paris require it.

Tunnelling began, using an assortment of roughnecks from far and wide, and many miners from the defunct Kent coalfields. Farthingole, the special township built to house them on Dover cliffs, was a rowdy place, compared to the Klondyke by a local journalist. Two male tunnellers founded the Mile Deep Club, but in general British diggers were strictly controlled when underground, forbidden to drink or smoke. To limit congestion, they were provided with 200 bicycles, on which they commuted to work under the Channel. After 'breakthrough', the British witnessed *la différence*. The French section was generally swisher and better-lit, it contained a shrine to St Barbara, the patron saint of miners, a 'cairn' of champagne bottles and the odd fag-end. The French tunnelling machines had girls' names: the British numbered theirs. With the tunnel complete, its newly installed smoke detectors needed to be tested. After much thought, a French steam train, built in 1900, was sent through it. What a science-fiction suggestion it would have seemed to that train's designer! Eurotunnel, proud of its hi-tech image, did not publicise this episode. The first press preview had a retro flavour too. As the sleek new Eurostar trains had yet to receive government safety clearance, the hacks were taken to France on a 1959 slam-door commuter train. To get safety clearance for the new train, 80 troubleshooting engineers took a momentous one-off Eurostar trip. The train had to be tested to the limit, so Kentish driver Alan Pears of Staplehurst reached a teacup-trembling 208mph (335km/h), still a UK record.

So, the Channel Rail link is a wonder of the world, and an eco-success story, passenger numbers having risen from two million to 17 million per year. But Britain has the oldest railway network in the world, and some of the most vocal villagers too. So it came to pass that those sleek Eurostar trains, which reach 186mph (299km/h), ran for the first seven years through the last manually operated level crossing in the country. For years, it seemed technically impossible to link Willesborough's crossing to an automated system, and all attempts to close the crossing met with stiff opposition from villagers, who refused to cross the track the long way around. And so crossing-keeper Bert Frolley kept his job until 2001, leaving his cosy hut to swing the white wooden gates across the track, and refilling the kerosene lamps on top of each gate. My cutting from the *Independent*, featuring a visit to Bert's hut by the crossing, describes its 'Baby Belling' stove, wireless and much-used toaster.

A VERY SURPRISING
HISTORY OF KENT TRAINS

1830–2011

The world's first passenger train service opened in 1830, between Canterbury and Whitstable. Thereafter, Kent has continued to be a battleground where trains compete with other modes of transport. The steam train reigned supreme for decades, but Kent, a prosperous county, took to the motor car enthusiastically, especially Walter Arnold of Paddock Wood. In 1896, he drove his Benz motor car at an insane 8mph (12.9km/h). A policeman on a bicycle pulled him over and arrested him; he received the world's first speeding ticket, and was fined a shilling at Tonbridge Assize Court.

In 1927, the 'RH&DR', or Romney, Hythe and Dymchurch Railway, 'the world's smallest railway', opened to great public excitement. But as the twentieth century progressed, car-mania was threatening train travel. This was dramatically so on the RH&DR, where cars would frequently hit trains on level crossings; the little trains always got knocked over. Down at Dover, a more serious threat was the growth of the 'car ferry'. Cars were being lifted by crane onto ferries for trips to France: 31,000 vehicles a year by 1939. At Lydd, cars could even drive onto aeroplanes for trips to France.

In 1936, the train fought back. An extraordinary Boat Train was introduced; not just a train that connected with ferry sailings, but a train which ran *onto rails on the deck of the ferry*. The ferry berthed in a special 'sea lock' at Dover to achieve this. Seawater was pumped out until the boat deck was at the right height for the train to steam onto the ship. A corresponding sea lock was constructed at Dunkirk. On this luxurious Night Ferry train, passengers, having checked into Customs at Victoria, could sleep all the way to Paris. Briefly in the 1960s, Kent's Boat Train ran all the way to Switzerland. By the time of the last Night Ferry train in 1980, its romantic 1930s *Compagnie Internationale des Wagons-Lit* carriages were the oldest in use in Britain. Older readers might like to know that the Night Ferry train was captured for posterity on TV in the 1974 *Steptoe and Son* Christmas special.

During the Second World War, a Kent train literally fought back. A German fighter, the Focke-Wulf 190, with its impressive rack of cannon, descended to strafe the 4.16p.m. Hastings to Ashford train, as it approached Lydd, on Romney Marsh. A direct hit on the engine failed to stop it or injure the driver, but debris shot up and hit the plane, which crashed, killing the pilot.

In 1962, Lord Beeching, born at Sheerness and educated at Maidstone Grammar School, brought shame on Kent with his draconian initiative to close a third of British branch lines. Although Kent was badly affected, he failed in his ambition to cut off Canterbury completely from the railway network.

Later in the 60s, the car struck another body blow to train travel through Kent, with the first 'roll-on, roll-off' car ferry. Despite the tragic flooding of one such ferry (the *Herald of Free Enterprise*) in 1987, with the loss of 193 passengers, 'Ro-Ro' seemed to have won Kent's transport battle, especially after the M2 opened in 1965. Until, that is, 1994, when the Channel Tunnel opened. Trains were soon running regularly at 186mph (299km/h), and in 2010 Siemens were awarded the contract to build the next generation of Eurostar trains, designed to run at 200mph (322km/h), as fast as a diving peregrine falcon.

With the opening in 2007 of the £5 billion high-speed line through Kent, the train can be said to have won its long and dramatic battle to be the most efficient and comfortable way to travel in Kent.

MARGATE'S ENIGMA

1835

The Shell Temple was discovered by accident in 1835.
Workmen digging a pond in the grounds of a Margate school
broke a small hole into an underground chamber.
Schoolmaster James Newlove lowered his son Joshua into
the chamber by rope and, candle in hand, he described a
sight as baffling as Stonehenge itself. Further excavation
revealed a curving, snake-like tunnel, 8ft (2.4m) high,
leading 70ft (21.3m) to a domed chamber that had once
admitted a beam of sunlight through a central aperture.

The whole temple is carved out of chalk and its walls
are decorated with four million shells, arranged in a
mind-boggling array of sacred symbols. Only Christianity
seems to be excluded. Iris, Osiris, Dionysus, the Tree of
Life, owls, turtles and Ganesha the Indian elephant god
adorn the tunnel as you journey to the central chamber,
which is decorated with the sun and moon. Pythagorean
geometry, classical symbolism, a pentagram, the Lotus and
Kabbalistic numbering have all allegedly been discovered
in the complex shell patterns. Gas lighting was installed
and soon blackened the shells, and rendered carbon-
dating impossible. Originally, as glimpsed by Joshua, the
background colour was the gold of yellow periwinkles, with
patterns in the pink, blue and ivory of other shells. Despite
the damp, they adhere firmly to the walls, although the glue
has defied analysis; it seems to contain fish oil.

This extraordinary place is so little known partly because, as a Victorian novelist said, it is in 'plebeian Margate'. Also, although English Heritage have now listed the temple, it has remained in private ownership since its discovery. Although it has always been blessed with sympathetic owners who have admitted the public, it has had little scholarly analysis.

When was it built? A detailed 1775 guide to Margate has no mention of it. Situated under open farmland when discovered in 1835, it was no mere aristocratic folly, being far too isolated from any large country house. A pale Victorian imitation, built in Surrey of just two types of shell, cost £60,000. You would expect such an amazing place as Margate's glittering cavern to have been mentioned in one of Kent's many travelogues, allowing English Heritage to identify its wealthy builder, but they are stumped.

Clearly, the temple was a secret place of ritual. Perhaps its random position was dictated by the sun entering the dome aperture at one of the solstices. Six enjoyably wild theories have been advanced:

1. *The Phoenicians built it in ancient times.* This 1980 theory sounds absurd, but their whole civilisation was built on distant sea trade: they visited Marseilles and Portugal, and the now silted-up Wantsum Channel, near the temple, was the first port of call for many visitors to England. Like the temple's iconography, Phoenician religion was a mixture of many Mediterranean civilisations. The Phoenicians got everywhere: St Augustine of Hippo spoke Phoenician, and fathered a child by a Phoenician woman.

2. *Freemasons built it.* The Masons are obsessed with secrecy and are also religious magpies, adopting symbols from all sorts of ancient traditions to lend gravitas to their proceedings.

3. *The Knights Templar built it.* Not as Da Vinci Code an idea as it seems. English Heritage own two important medieval Templar properties in Kent. Margate is easily accessible to returning and departing Crusader Templars. The Pope banned their order because of alleged secret heretical rituals. These have never been fully discovered, but involved an initiation with sexual overtones. Recently opened Vatican records of Templar interrogations contain several confessions of the 'obscene kiss', the kissing by a man of another's behind. Male and female genitalia adorn the Margate temple. Perhaps, therefore, it is medieval and was sealed up when the Pope banned the Knights Templar in 1312.

4. *Eighteenth-century poet Alexander Pope built it* as a 'Grotto' in Twickenham, but sailed it down the Thames in sections to Margate. Academic Ruby Haslam argues this theory in her likeable 2009 book *Reality and Imagery*, but it seems more outlandish than any of the above, although not quite as unbelievable as the final two theories.

5. *It marks a meteorite landing.*

6. *It was built to house the Ark of the Covenant.*

As long as the archaeologists fail to date Margate's enigma, we can all continue to enjoy these excursions of the imagination. Long may they be puzzled.

HOW TO BE A RECLUSE, BY CHARLES DARWIN

1842

Darwin lived at Down House, near Sevenoaks, for 40 years (1842–82). There he researched the specimens gathered on his famous HMS *Beagle* voyages, wrote the *Origin of Species* and four other major works. The *Origin*, at 600 pages long, took 20 years to write. It was originally four times longer, but Darwin rushed out a shorter book because other scientists were beginning to publish their own versions of the theory of evolution.

Although tourists from all over the world now visit the famous study at Down House, the father of evolutionary theory hammered out much of his analysis in the garden. Here, he had his grassy 'thinking walk' made. He paced it several times a day, counting the laps by picking up a flint at one end and dropping it at the other. These perambulations were necessitated by the scientist's chronic illness; he was under strict doctor's orders not to slave at the desk for long each day. It's now thought that he had Chagas' disease, contracted while living in remote South American natives' huts. There, at night, the 'large fat assassin bug of the pampas' dropped from the thatch to bite the sleepers below. A zoologist I met was shown a jar of the bugs. They were so dangerous that he was told not to touch the brass lid of the jar in case the beasts punctured it. Another reason, apart from his ailment, for Darwin to be in the garden so much was that he had turned it into an open-air laboratory, with 29 types of cabbage, a weed-patch which he grew specifically to observe natural selection at work, and a 'worm-stone', a boulder which he measured gradually sinking into the earth: evidence of the behaviour of worms.

All this made him easy to glimpse from the road. Soon after moving in with his wife Emma, he wrote: 'the publicity of this place is intolerable', but Victorian West Kent was a hard place to hide. With scientific determination, however, Darwin succeeded in sinking from view. He moved the front door, had high flint walls built around the garden, and actually lowered the lane outside the house. He informed his wife that even a short visit from strangers overexcited him so much that he experienced violent fits of shivering, usually vomiting as well. As his research time became all the more precious, he announced that he had 'lost the power of becoming deeply attached to anyone', except his much-loved wife and ten children, and could not receive callers. Darwin gradually acquired an aura of utter inaccessibility. He recorded with intense satisfaction that a German magazine profile described him living in a remote Kent house 'which can only be reached up a perilous mule-track'. It is quite possible that, without this determination to remain private, his *Origin of Species* might never have been completed.

WELLINGTON AND THE OLD SOLDIER

1847

The strange post of Lord Warden of the Cinque Ports has for many years been a sinecure, a way to reward those who have served the country. It comes with an official residence, Walmer Castle, near Deal. Although not all incumbents took up residence, the Duke of Wellington did: he was to die there, in his favourite armchair, having just said yes to a cup of tea.

The Iron Duke was a soldiers' soldier, as tough as his men. After a fatherless childhood, neglected by his mother, the Duke evolved his notable reserve and a carapace of laconic wit. 'I've lost my leg!' said a subordinate after a shell-burst. 'My God, so you have,' was the Duke's reply. He once opposed soldiers cheering as 'too close to an expression of opinion'. But he felt deeply for his men. After Waterloo, he refused to be congratulated, so distraught was he at the loss of soldiers. In the evening, he broke down in tears.

A little-known tale from an obscure Victorian history of Deal illustrates the Duke's inner character well. Long after the fall of Napoleon, Wellington received a letter from a retired sergeant who was lamenting his lack of pension. The Duke summoned the old soldier to a meeting and said briskly, 'Take the place of gardener at Walmer Castle, 28 shillings a week, a house, and all that.' 'But I know very little about gardening,' the veteran replied. The Duke answered, 'Nor do I! Go and take your place at once!' On arrival at Walmer, the sergeant was welcomed and placed in a comfortable cottage. The Duke also avoided all attempts at gratitude by the sergeant, who would rise at 6a.m. and stand in the way of Wellington's regular morning walk. The sergeant had barely doffed his hat when the Duke sped past with 'How d'ye do, how d'ye do?'

KENT'S STRANGEST CRICKET

1847 ONWARDS

Somewhat predictably, Kent cricket experts insist that the game originated in Kent, and not, as is usually claimed, in Hampshire. In Kent's defence, stool-ball, cricket's ancestor, which was once thought extinct, is still played at many locations in the county. Straight-arm bowling was certainly invented in Kent, in a desperate bid to beat Surrey, in 1798.

Antiquity aside, Kent's cricket reigns supreme in sheer strangeness.

Most famously, the St Lawrence Ground in Canterbury had, from 1847 until 2005, a tree on the pitch. Although it blew down in 2005, Kent Cricket Club replaced it with a young tree planted in 1999 in anticipation of the original lime's demise. This lime tree is the source of certain rules, unique to this ground, including an official, MCC-approved score if the tree was hit: 4. Only three players in history managed to hit a six by getting the ball clean over the original tree and to the boundary.

Almost as rare as the tree was the pre-war match in West Kent where a ball went through the stumps without dislodging the bails (the horizontal stick of wood on top of the stumps). This should be impossible, as the gap is just 2in (5cm), less than the diameter of a ball, but in certain atmospheric conditions, it happens. Dorothy Gardner records the West Kent instance in her rambling, hard-to-find book, *Kentish Pilgrimage*. The only other recorded instance seems to be a 2004 report from Sunderland, which was photographed.

In 1824, the Ramsgate Harbourmaster, a Captain Martin, began the traditional annual cricket match on the Goodwin Sands at low tide. This long and treacherous sandbank, 'the ship-swallower', is mentioned as far back as Shakespeare. Victorian cricketers played there in top hat and tails, making for some surreal early photographs. The tradition lasted until 2003. It was an absurdly dangerous eccentricity, as a BBC film crew discovered in 2006. In their attempt to film a re-enactment of the match on the Sands, they were caught out by the tide and had to be rescued by the Ramsgate Lifeboat.

The Goodwin match, far out at sea, demonstrates the Kentish determination to play against *any* odds. Similarly, the Victorian Vicar of Benenden, an excellent batsman, hearing of evangelical disapproval of Sunday matches, insisted on playing Sunday cricket in full vestments. Even if the performance of Kent cricket has not always been world class, its spirit is world-beating.

THE RAMSGATE MADMAN WHO DESIGNED BIG BEN

1852

Victorian Gothic architecture is back in fashion. Once-reviled buildings which were nearly demolished, such as St Pancras Station, are now lovingly restored. Augustus Pugin, the father of the Victorian Gothic Revival, lived in an elaborate medieval-fantasy building in Ramsgate. With its dazzling wallpapers, bright hanging tapestries and glowing tiles, it sounds like the set for the 1938 Technicolor Robin Hood film. There was even a chapel, with a resident Italian Catholic chaplain.

The whole complex, which is still inhabited, was Pugin's favourite building, the only one on which he never had to scrimp or compromise.

Forever in overdrive, Pugin was a draughtsman by 14, running a business by 19, and dead at 40, having designed scores of buildings, and written books insisting that architecture must be 'a romantic moral force'. He hated to see mankind turned into drones by the industrial revolution, so he loved things to be made by hand.

He fell in love as easily as he wept: often. Here he is in his prime, as described by an assistant, Hardman Powell: 'a massive forehead, quick, pale grey eyes, a sonorous trumpet voice and long dark hair'[1]. When working well, he sang opera in a loud baritone, swearing filthily when things went awry. He

---

1. Quoted in *God's Architect*, by Rosemary Hill (Allen Lane, London, 2007), p.325

habitually dressed in a greasy sailor's jacket, with loose pilot trousers, jackboots and 'a wideawake hat'. Understandably, he was challenged when boarding a first-class train carriage: 'You must be mistaken, sir!' said a passenger. 'Yes,' Pugin quipped, 'I thought I was in the presence of a gentleman.' The two chatted amicably for the rest of the journey. He frequently took to sea, and supplemented his income by getting salvage from Kentish wrecks. 'So you see the sort of man he was,' said John Betjeman in a 1952 wireless talk, 'unconventional, downright and humorous ... an intense individualist who loved people.' Pugin's greatest work was his co-design for the Houses of Parliament. Although architect Charles Barry claimed most of the credit, Pugin, with his incredible speed and versatility, designed and oversaw most of the interior, from the great throne in the Lords, down to elaborate letterboxes and door-handles.

As his final illness, probably syphilis, affected his body and mind, he still overworked, slaving on panelling and carpets for the long-running Parliament project. To the despair of his third wife Jane, 6a.m. until 10p.m. was his normal shift, but he was increasingly plagued by visions and 'mind mists'. As he slipped in and out of insanity, a committee of his friends decided to commit him to 'Bedlam', the dreadful Bethlem Royal Hospital. Just before he went there, a letter from Charles Barry arrived, imploring help with the final problem at Westminster: a clock. Pugin rose to the challenge and, as he wrote in one of his last letters, 'never worked so hard'. Of his bell-tower design, he said, 'it is beautiful and I am the whole machinery of the clock', meaning, he worked so hard that, in his madness, he almost became Big Ben. How fitting that, with his great desire to benefit his fellow man, his final design was the most-loved building in Britain.

Happily, at the end of his life, his wife got him out of Bedlam and back home. As they sat together in the garden at Ramsgate, he uttered almost his last words to her: 'It's a beautiful place, is it not? It's all yours, my dear wife.'

THE SHOPKEEPER
WHO HELPED TO REWRITE
HUMAN HISTORY
1854

It all started when Ightham resident Benjamin Harrison was taken, as a boy, to the Great Exhibition in Hyde Park. It fired his interest in nature study and on the way home his dad took him to the Geological Museum at the Royal Academy in Piccadilly. That was it: Benjamin started collecting fossils back in Ightham and never stopped. He lived in Ightham for all of his 83 years.

One day he saw a man, Bob Jessop, draining a bog and saying, 'Here's a queer stone.' Harrison concluded that these queer-shaped stones with hand-axes and flint blades must be man-made. He collected over 10,000 'eoliths' (implements made by early man), and kept them in labelled boxes. He was often laughed at, but took solace from a book by a Boucher de Perches, *Antiquites Celtique et Antediluviennes* (1847), which illustrated 1,600 such stones. Even when Perches found a human jaw among flint tools, he was ridiculed by churchmen. The non-academic pedigree of these men of science is interesting. Just as Darwin trained in theology and Einstein was a patent clerk, Harrison was a shopkeeper and de Perches was a Customs Officer.

Harrison is a little-known figure who does not even feature in the *Dictionary of National Biography*. He has only recently been given his due in books such as *Kent in Prehistoric Times* (2005) by Paul Ashbee, who believed that

Harrison's unstudied notebooks, in Maidstone Museum, will eventually prove a treasure trove. As a result, any map of Ancient Kent is, almost comically, covered with find records at Ightham as if it was a prehistoric conurbation; it's just where Harrison and his friends hunted eoliths for 50 years.

TIME AT THE SPEED
OF LIGHT
1855

In Deal, they sell tea-towels of the Goodwin Sands. They are peppered with shipwrecks and are mentioned with dread in both *The Merchant of Venice* and *Moby Dick*. Even the Goodwin Sands Lightship is wrecked there, still visible at low tide.

But this treacherous sandbank off the coast has a positive side. It protects a calm channel, 'The Downs', which provided an ideal place for sailing ships to anchor while they took on last-minute supplies: drinking water, fruit and so on. Lord Nelson, doubtless like many others, nipped ashore for a night of love – with Lady Hamilton – before he went on one long voyage. You can still stay in their bedroom at the Royal Hotel. For centuries, Deal's economy was kept afloat by supplying ships 'resting' offshore. The older houses have cut-off corners, to allow huge carts of victuals to heave through the narrow old streets. In a symbol of Deal's link to the sea, the Mayor carries a silver oar on official occasions. Bizarrely, when he visits ships, he becomes, automatically, an admiral.

Those ships anchored in the Downs before long voyages needed to set their chronometers accurately. As Dava Sobel's bestselling book *Longitude* vividly explained, the calculation of longitude by matching the exact time to the positions of planets was a hugely important breakthrough by John Harrison, an eighteenth-century Yorkshireman. At last, mariners could fix their position accurately anywhere on the globe, but only if they set their chronometers exactly, before they left. In Deal, a cannon used to be fired, like Edinburgh's one o'clock gun, but, because sound travels 'slowly', cannon-fire did not give an exact time, especially in windy weather. Strange 'chrono-maps' were produced in Edinburgh, showing the exact time, a few seconds after 1p.m., in various parts of the city when the gun was fired. Then, in 1829, a Scottish admiral, Robert Wauchope, invented an instant time signal for ships: the Timeball. A metal sphere, pneumatically powered, atop a tower, ascends a pole just before 1p.m., and drops at 1p.m. precisely. Time is thus transmitted to ships at the speed of light, not sound: 300 million metres (984 million feet) per second, not 300 metres (984 feet) per second. Deal's Timeball, built in 1855, was connected by telegraph to the Greenwich Observatory, the home of Greenwich Mean Time, and of the Prime Meridian, longitude zero.

When wireless sets started to emit time signals, the Timeballs of the world were doomed, and only a few now survive, including ones in Sydney Harbour, Cape Town and New York. After years of neglect, Deal's Timeball is now fully restored. Connected to the atomic clock at Rugby, it drops at exactly 1p.m. Nelson would be pleased.

CAN YOU PLAN
HAPPINESS?

1860

Utopia. Probably more than any Englishman, William Morris is associated with the aspiration to create an idealised world. A passionate lover of the Middle Ages and a pioneer science-fiction writer, he was a fireball of abilities. Poet, painter, novelist, weaver, translator of Icelandic sagas, book designer, the list goes on. His wallpaper motifs are still in use. He co-founded British Socialism, refreshed the Gothic Revival, founded the Society for the Protection of Ancient Buildings, and his thinking inspired both the National Trust and the early environmental movement. Educated at Marlborough and Oxford, he inherited much wealth.

In Kent, at Bexleyheath, Morris created his dream house in 1860, the Red House. It was a new house built on old ideals, and it cost an eye-watering £4,000 (£2 million today). Using local red brick, Morris made a house designed for human harmony (assisted by four live-in servants and a nanny). It was to be the 'Happy Home of Arthurian legend', and Arthurian murals decorated the interior. Morris, like his hero King Arthur, strived to inspire England to nobler ideals.

Every aspect of Red House life reflected those ideals. Guests were collected from the station in a specially designed horse-drawn wagon with leather curtains. A covered garden seat was called the Pilgrims Rest. The

Morrises wore bohemian clothing and Morris presided over the carefully planned rooms with larger-than-life hospitality. One dinner guest recalled him bursting out of the cellar, mid-evening, smiling broadly with bottles of wine under each arm. Morris's like-minded friends formed 'The Pre-Raphaelite Brotherhood'. These men loved Malory's *Morte D'Arthur*, Tennyson's *Idylls of the King* and medieval craftsmanship. One of them, Edward Burne-Jones, installed a stained-glass window in the Red House, on the theme of perfect love. Another, the poet and painter Dante Gabriel Rossetti, called the home 'more a poem than a house'. Morris agreed. He hoped that he had created, in a deep sense, 'the beautiful-est place on earth'. Now a National Trust property, it is, outwardly, a shrine to domestic bliss.

Life and love in the Red House were in reality bittersweet, far from Utopia. All of the Brotherhood were posh, but fell in love with commoners: maids, cleaners, etc. This was because their ideal of womanhood was Guinevere, or some other idealised heroine from a noble myth, such as Isolde. Working-class women could be moulded into the ideal more easily than stroppy, educated women of the same class. So, Brotherhood members strenuously educated their women in their own style. Their conduct inspired Shaw's *Pygmalion*. One member, novelist Ford Madox Ford, concealed his trashy lover from all his friends for two years until he had polished her up. He then married her but, unsurprisingly, after entering society she became an alcoholic. The reality of womanhood up close provided some shocks. Ruskin, godfather of the Brotherhood, ran from his honeymoon bedroom in horror at his first sight of pubic hair.

William Morris's wife Jane, the lady of the Red House, was a groom's daughter, spotted in a London crowd aged 17, and plucked from working-class obscurity into an upper-class mythological playground. Her glossy black hair and striking looks are symbols of Victorian fantasy-art. But in old age she reflected that she had never loved Morris, despite conceiving two children by him. For a girl of her station, she explained, a marriage offer from a rich toff like Morris simply could not be refused. The mischievous Irishman George Bernard Shaw, who knew the Morrises, observed that Jane's function was merely to be beautiful. The Brotherhood's idealism was somewhat confused; Morris's close friend Rossetti had a long-standing affair with Jane during her marriage to Morris. Rossetti's own unfortunate wife, Lizzie, had first been talent-spotted as a potential Guinevere while she was doing a window display in a London hat shop. Probably as ill prepared as any of the Brotherhood's muses, Lizzie became a drug addict and died young, of an overdose.

Morris famously insisted that, in your house, you must have only things that are useful or beautiful. At the Red House, he wanted this artistic idealism to be matched with ideal love. He failed, and more ideal marriages probably abounded in the naff, aesthetically crass new villas going up all around him in Bexleyheath. In defence of the Red House, his children loved it, especially when they were playing in the garden.

DICKENS' GREAT LOVE EXPOSED BY A TRAIN CRASH

1865

Friday, 9 June 1865 was a clear, hot day. At 2.30p.m., a train left Folkestone for London Charing Cross. Charles Dickens, a married man, sat discreetly in the front carriage with Nelly Ternan, his mistress and the love of his life. It is now thought that he had already fathered a child by Nelly. Dickens was an international literary superstar, having written *David Copperfield*, *Oliver Twist*, *A Christmas Carol* and *Great Expectations*. His admirers included Queen Victoria and Dostoevsky. In his bag, he carried the partly finished *Our Mutual Friend*, and his customary brandy flask.

Near Staplehurst some railway workers forgot to signal that they had interrupted the track. In the ensuing derailment, ten people died. Dickens owed his safety to his discreet strategy of taking the first and emptiest carriage, which jumped over the gap in the rails. Most of the train plunged down an embankment. Dickens administered brandy and sympathy to the injured, and prints were soon on sale of this pillar of Victorian society going about this charitable work. But his main concern was to conceal Nelly's presence. He refused to attend the inquest, and somehow Nelly escaped unnamed, but one female survivor was recorded as refusing to give her name, and Dickens' grand passion was soon to seep out among his immediate circle.

Nelly, an actress, had captivated Dickens a decade earlier,

when he was 45, and she just 18. Opinionated, literary, politicised and feisty, she was everything his wife Catherine was not, and, for good measure, she was Kentish, born in his beloved Rochester. The author set Nelly up in a series of houses and visited her under assumed names, several times a week. For a while, she was housed in northern France, probably Boulogne or Paris: the fateful train was a service which connected with a ferry from France. The love lasted until Dickens' death, and, despite a strenuous cover-up which involved rushing him to another house, it is now known that Nelly was with him when he suffered his fatal stroke in 1870.

Soon after the train crash, he had indiscreetly written to the Charing Cross stationmaster asking for the jewellery which Nelly lost in the crash. There was a lot of it, all gold, and all given by the novelist. This loving habit was to end his marriage. In 1858, Mrs Dickens took delivery of a fine bracelet inscribed to Nelly and the marriage was over.

Mysteries remain. Where was Nelly's house in France, where the baby was probably born, and who cared for her child; did the child live into old age? Several people purporting to be the child of Nelly and Charles have come forward over the years.

What became of Nelly? She married George Robinson, a Margate schoolmaster, in 1876. They had children – the last of whom, a daughter, died senile in 1973. George predeceased Nelly, who lived quietly on into the twentieth century. In 1907, she had a successful breast operation for cancer and in 1911 she joined the Suffragettes. An admiring young niece marvelled at Auntie Nelly's unconventional ways and humour, recalling this self-deprecation: 'I'm the ugly sister, with a complexion like a copper saucepan and a figure like an oak tree.' The niece, Helen, was told by her mother, 'Don't bother Nell about Dickens, she doesn't wish to remember those days, it makes her so sad.' Yet one day Nell privately showed Helen a picture of Gads Hill Place,

Dickens' mansion in Rochester, murmuring that she had been there 'many times'. In 1914, a few months before an armageddon started which her old lover could not have imagined, she died, aged 75. She took her secrets to the grave, and never told her children that she was anything more than a theatrical acquaintance of Dickens.

BRITAIN'S ONLY GREEN PILLAR BOX

1866

It was Anthony Trollope, novelist and Post Office official, who suggested the idea of the UK pillar box. He had seen a version of the idea in Paris. Rather than letters being given to the local postmaster, they could be left at collection points. Many designs were tried out, including a disastrous one devised by a Parliamentary Committee. Strangely, there are 150 different versions of these exotic pieces of street furniture surviving in Britain. All of them, except one, are red. And it's in Rochester.

Organisations such as the Council for the Protection of Rural England and the Letter Box Study Group fiercely defend our box diversity. These are the experts who know about surviving red boxes in Gibraltar, Tel Aviv and Kuwait. And they have a proper reverence for the red Ramsgate pillar box, apparently unremarkable, but bearing the lettering, 'EVIII'. It is one of very few boxes from the 326-day reign of Edward VIII, who abdicated to be with his American lover, Wallis Simpson. Among these box experts, architect John Penfold (1828–1909) is regarded as the Leonardo of pillar box design. His 1866 octagonal box with the beautifully playful acorn on top is known simply as 'The Penfold'. Replicas of it exist from Scotland to Singapore and there remain several original Penfolds around. However, only the Rochester High Street Penfold retains the original livery intended by its architect: green, with gold lettering and mouldings.

And, yes, the cartoon character Danger Mouse's companion Penfold was named after the pillar box designer. As you will no doubt recall, the two crusaders used to meet in a Baker Street pillar box. But do not mention this connection to members of the Letter Box Study Group because – *quelle horreur!* – the cartoon box is not a Penfold, but a more practical larger, later box.

KENT'S MOST
USEFUL VICAR
1867

In 1967, on Sunday, 22 October, a strange lunch was held at Dymchurch vicarage, on the lonely shoreline where Romney Marsh meets the sea. Those present were the Vicar of Dymchurch, the Archbishop of Canterbury Michael Ramsey, the Bailiff of Romney Marsh and Monsieur Collett, the French Consul from Folkestone. This wonderfully Dickensian guest list was gathered together because they had just attended the unveiling of a citation which recalled a little-known event from 100 years before.

On a stormy Sunday in January 1867, the French lugger *Courier de Dieppe*, a three-masted fishing boat, was grounded off Dymchurch. As the tempest battered the ship, it began to break up, watched by an anxious crowd, which included many fishermen onshore. It was heartbreakingly impossible to help the crew of the ship, although it was only 60ft (18.3m) away. Rescue ropes, repeatedly shot from a mortar cannon onshore, failed to reach the men, and the master, cabin boy and a seaman were all swept off the wreck and drowned in sight of the crowd. Only the ship's mate remained, clinging to the rigging. The Vicar of Dymchurch, 39-year-old Charles Cobb – predecessor of the fictional swashbuckling vicar, Dr Syn – heard the mortar-fire over breakfast at the vicarage and hurried to the shore, just in time to see the heroic action of Dymchurch coastguard Jean Batist. Wearing a cork jacket, and secured by a rope attached to a beach groyne, Batist swam out towards the wreck. Battered by choppy waves and unable to reach it, he was dragged back onshore.

What happened next brings a tear to the eye as I recount it. The vicar began to take off most of his clothes and wade into the sea. The crowd, a Victorian report said, 'remonstrated with him to desist', especially as he did not have a rope attaching him to the shore and 'it was blowing a strong gale from the South by East, with a heavy sea running'. The Reverend Cobb reached the mate, and Batist was so inspired that he swam out again with a line and reached the wreck. All three men were hauled back together. Queen Victoria gave Cobb the gold Albert Medal for Lifesaving (the forerunner of the George Cross). Batist received the bronze medal. Cobb ended his life as vicar of Rainham, Kent, and is buried in the churchyard there. His physical fitness stood him in good stead, as he lived to be 90, and died in 1918.

THE HIDDEN GENIUS

1871

Nobody, in general, has heard of John Herschel, because his interests were so broad, and his speculations so ahead of his time. For 30 years at his Regency home, Collingwood House, Hawkhurst, near Tonbridge, he quietly transformed a bewildering number of disciplines; evidenced by over 10,000 letters to him which survive from experts all over the world. In the same period, 50 miles (80.5km) away across Kent, Darwin was similarly working away at Down House to transform science. Herschel was a major influence on Darwin, having written about a theory of 'the evolution of organic forms'.

As the only child of William Herschel, John could not be a slouch. William built gigantic telescopes, coined the word asteroid, discovered Neptune, infra-red light and the fact that coral is an animal, not a plant. He also wrote 20 symphonies. He did 'let the side down' amusingly by insisting that huge-headed aliens lived on the sun. John was greatly influenced by his father's sister Caroline, whom diarist Fanny Burney called 'very little, very gentle, and unhackneyed'. Caroline discovered eight comets and has a lunar crater named after her.

Armed with these influences, and having worked with computer pioneer Charles Babbage at Cambridge University, Herschel was reluctant to get distracted by a paid job. Only after he fathered his eleventh child did he reluctantly accept the post of Master of the Mint in London. This was a disaster. With his wild, mad professor hair and raffish dress, recorded in photographs, he must have cut an eccentric figure in London. Although he radically reformed the Mint, working away from home and family gave him a nervous breakdown. He was soon happily back at Collingwood House, where he went on to father, at 63, a twelfth child and write eight books, including a pioneer work on probability theory and a translation of Homer's *Iliad*. During his Kent years, when skies were darker than now, he also named the moons of Saturn and Uranus. His catalogue of over 10,000 double stars might seem nerdy, but, in realising that the distortion effects observed in such stars held the key to understanding light, he was pioneering what came to be called quantum physics. One modern scientist has written that Herschel was practising 'the astronomy of the future'. Incredibly – his Scottish wife Margaret must have been good at keeping the children quiet (nine boys and three girls) – he also wrote an Admiralty text on meteorology and a philosophy book. This was translated into several languages and influenced the heavyweight utilitarian philosopher John Stuart Mill. His contributions to chemistry and mathematics were also important (but completely over my head). As practical as his telescope-making father, John Herschel pioneered the use of the camera, inventing the words 'negative', 'snapshot' and 'photographer'. He would have been pleased to know that his son, another William, would pioneer colour photography (and invent fingerprinting). As a result of John's botanical studies into scent, he planted exotic trees, some of which still thrive at Collingwood.

When Herschel died, there was widespread agreement on where to bury him: next to Isaac Newton in Westminster Abbey. Perhaps because we live in an age of specialists, John Herschel, Kent's hidden genius, has slipped into obscurity.

VAN GOGH, MATHS TEACHER

1876

The publication of the complete *Van Gogh Letters* in 2009 was an event which not many could enjoy. In their wooden box, strong enough to hold all seven volumes, with the artist's sketches – he decorated most of his letters – the price tag was £450. But for the first time, buried in *Volume II*, Vincent's letters from Ramsgate were presented with his sketches of the place, and even a photo of the Ramsgate seaweed which he sent to his brother Theo.

In 1876, aged 23, Van Gogh spent a year living in Ramsgate. It is strange to think of him teaching 14-year-olds in a class in Thanet. The classroom looked out upon the sea and he was sure that 'many a boy will never forget the view from that window'. During the Battle of Britain, there must have been some men in their late seventies who could have recalled, 'Yes, I had a weird maths teacher in Ramsgate, Dutch bloke, a bit intense.' The pupils would have liked his habit of taking the boys out on unscheduled walks when it was fine. Once, he made a massive sandcastle with them.

Just ten years later, he would settle in Arles, Provence, painting pictures, many of which are now worth over £50 million. In Arles, a young girl, Jeanne Calment, sold him coloured pencils in her dad's shop. That girl just happened to live to 122, and recalled in 1995 that Van Gogh was 'dirty, badly dressed and disagreeable'. Tragically, he was to die at 37, unaware of the scale of his future distinction.

Remarkably, the complete letters show that Vincent did not need the light of Provence to be inspired. Fellow painter-of-light, J.M.W. Turner, loved the light in Margate and Thanet, insisting it was better than anything he'd ever seen in Italy. Indeed, his *Fighting Temeraire* (voted 'Britain's Favourite Painting' in 2005) depicts a scene off northeast Kent.

Turner's view of Deal in a storm was painted from a boat offshore, and is a celebration of Thanet light. (It ought to be much better known, but this publicly owned treasure hangs in the offices of Deal Town Hall. Attempts to see it are stonewalled by officials.) Van Gogh similarly raved about 'the beautiful, natural state' of the light over this coast. His descriptions of everyday natural Kent are scintillating to read, because this was the man who gave mankind a new way of seeing, a baptism in coloured paint. He wrote of one walk, 'through fields of young wheat and hedgerows of hawthorn, a high, steep wall of sand and stone, old gnarled hawthorn bushes, their black and grey lichen-covered stems and branches all bent to one side by the wind, and the ground, covered with chalk and shells. To the right was the sea, as calm as a pond, reflecting the delicate grey sky where the sun was setting.'

It dawned on Van Gogh that Ramsgate had 'something very singular', a 'special quality, that one notices the sea in everything'. A storm in May seems to have been as important to him as Turner's storm 10 miles (16.1km) away and half a century earlier. Ramsgate's elevated position gave the Dutch artist the sort of theatrical overall view of the tempest which was impossible in the Netherlands: the 'yellowish light', 'huge dark clouds from which one saw the rain come slanting down in lit streaks'. And there is something hallucinogenically real about this passage: 'The wind blew the dust from the small white path on the cliff into the sea and shook the blossoming hawthorn bushes. Behind me, fields of young green wheat.'

Later, in the dark dawn, from his attic window, he heard

a nightingale and a lark singing across each other with, in the distance, the light of the lighthouse and a guard-ship.

During his time as a Ramsgate teacher, Van Gogh was happy, and spiritually satisfied. He went to church often, and loved the singing so much that he sent an English hymnal to his brother. He rounded off his magical coastal sojourn by walking from his home in Spencer Square to London, a distance of some 75 miles (121km).

In Ramsgate, of all places, Van Gogh was inspired.

THE GHOST WHO ENDED A FRIENDSHIP

1879

Lord Halifax (1839–1934) was an aristocrat and leading churchman, who dedicated most of his life to church unity. He came from a long line of powerful, intelligent establishment figures; his son was Foreign Secretary and Viceroy of India. But for decades Halifax quietly gathered accounts from people who had seen ghosts. At the end of his life, they were made available by an obscure publisher in a limited edition as *Lord Halifax's Ghost Book*. That first edition is now much sought after by collectors, as a treasure trove of Victorian paranormal oral history.

This tale came from the household of a major in the Royal Engineers, the splendidly named Alured de Vere Brooke, who in 1879 went to stay with old friends at Wrotham House, near Sevenoaks. It was a cold autumn day. The major and his wife were shown to their rooms, which were upstairs, at the end of a long passage, in a distant wing of the house. Although a fire was crackling in the bedroom grate, the room seemed extraordinarily cold to Mrs Brooke, who arranged extra blankets for the bed.

The Brookes dressed for dinner and went downstairs. Their hosts knew how to 'live it up', and dancing lasted until after 2a.m. Having retired to bed, tired though they were, they could not sleep. It was 'horribly cold' in spite of the fire. They assumed the mattresses were damp from disuse. Nothing supernatural entered their heads on this first visit.

Next spring, Mrs Brooke returned for a week's stay, with her serving maid. The major was away on military service. This time Mrs Brooke had asked in advance for the bedding to be aired and for a large fire. Her maid was to sleep in the adjacent room. During the evening, she told her mistress that the servants had suggested they were in haunted rooms. Mrs Brooke asked her hostess about this, but received an evasive reply. Still her room was cold but she fell into a light sleep as the fire crackled gently.

At midnight, she awoke, hearing a clock chime the hour. She was freezing. Footsteps approached down the long passage and stopped outside her door. The door opened noiselessly, and in walked a man who, by the firelight, seemed to be wearing a grey suit trimmed with silver and a cocked hat. Mrs Brooke wrote in her account that she now had trouble breathing, such was her terror. The figure walked to the window, paused, uttered 'a horrid little laugh' and left the room. In the morning, Brooke assumed she had experienced a dreadful nightmare. She asked her maid to spend the next night on the sofa in the same room. The figure came again, with the same diabolical little laugh.

Lord Halifax printed the separate testimony of the maid, confirming the apparition. In the morning, Mrs Brooke told her hostess that she was leaving immediately and challenged her over the figure. The hostess admitted that it had been appearing for over 80 years in that room, but never did any harm! At this, Mrs Brooke wrote, the friendship was over. Mrs Brooke learned later that an ancestor of the hostess had murdered his brother and thrown the body out of that window. A portrait in the house showed him in the very clothes which she had seen.

THE DARK SIDE OF AN ARCHBISHOP

1883–96

As you enter Canterbury Cathedral, the first monument that strikes you is the huge Gothic-canopied tomb of Edward Benson, Archbishop of Canterbury for 13 years (1883–96). It is the size of a truck. Classical figures mourn over the alabaster figure of Benson, and Latin inscriptions sing his praises. In life, he had been painted by the society portraitist Herkomer, who emphasised this holy image: Benson gazes piously, with the flowing white hair of a prophet. He holds a Bible.

The truth is darker. When he had been a public school headmaster, he believed in beating sin out of his pupils. One was beaten daily for weeks on end; another recalled how Benson would turn white (with rage or excitement?) when flogging boys. They hated him for this, and for his habit of toadying to titled parents.

Taking a shine to his 11-year-old cousin, he sat her on his knee and, disturbingly, told her that they would be married. On her seventeenth birthday, they were. He bullied her so much, emotionally and physically, that she lived in fear of him, and was in a turmoil of remorse after his death, fearing that she had not done enough for him. She found happiness eventually as a lesbian, pouring out her feelings in a revealing (unpublished) diary.

As Archbishop, he was famed for two things: his interest in the minutiae of ritual, and his zeal for sending missionaries overseas. He had six children; one son referred to his inability to relax as 'pathological', and recalled him preaching that 'irresponsible enjoyment' weakened 'moral fibre'. Another son described the Archbishop's religion as 'not of a mystic, but of a disciplinary type' and wondered whether his father 'ever really loved'. He was certainly no barrel of laughs as a family man, and his children were impacted in various ways. Hugh Benson became a devoted Roman Catholic, rising to be a monsignor, the ultimate rebellion. E.F. Benson wrote the *Mapp and Lucia* satires on provincial snobbery, as well as heated stories about love between schoolboys, while poor Maggie became insane. Intriguingly, none of the six children ever married.

Understandably, the character of this Archbishop puzzled church historian P.G. Maxwell-Stuart, who assumed that this 'unpleasant man' was, as Archbishop, simply acting the part, enjoying the status of his post, with its two palaces and retinue of servants. To the end, Benson inspired fear; when he died, sitting upright in his pew, he was left untouched until the service was over.

OPENING A CRUSADER'S TOMB

1892

They chose a quiet time to open the tomb of Hubert Walter. That Monday morning in Canterbury Cathedral, 10 March 1892, only seven officials attended the event: six senior clerics and a historian. The press were not invited, and the little-known astonishing report of what was found remains buried away in Volume 61 of the *Transactions of the Kent Archaeological Society* (1893). Hubert Walter, familiar to many as the good-guy senior minister in Robin Hood films, was one of the most remarkable men in history.

All his life, he was mocked for his lack of formal education, but this Norfolk lad was a brilliant politician and a formidable warrior. Described as handsome and unusually tall for the time, he was the trusted senior adviser of three very different kings: Henry II, Richard the Lionheart and John. They were stormy, violent characters. As Chief Justice, Walter reformed the law, overseeing the introduction of the jury system; as Chancellor, he overhauled taxation and moderated regal excesses; as Archbishop of Canterbury, he healed internal strife so skilfully that the Pope made him his legate. Kings trusted him absolutely and he had two spells of running the country during royal absence.

As a Crusader, he led Richard the Lionheart's forces at the siege of Acre, and personally led attacks on Saladin's camp. King Richard was a butcher; the massacre of 3,000 Muslim prisoners being only one of his atrocities. When Richard fell ill, Walter took the opportunity to make peace with Saladin, eventually negotiating shared Muslim/Christian access to Bethlehem and Jerusalem. The two men were kindred spirits; Saladin, an Iraqi, was respected even by contemporary Western chroniclers as a chivalrous soldier, a brilliant commander and an innovative administrator: a Muslim version of Walter. In his repeated negotiations, the Englishman must have drawn unfavourable comparisons between Richard and Saladin. Walter's conduct also implies a respect for other religions, and an eclectic spirituality, as his tomb-opening was to prove.

This brings us back to that Victorian Monday, with snow-light flooding through the cathedral windows (records show that it had snowed daily for the previous 12 days).

The first surprise, revealed by a lighted taper, was that there was another, hermetically sealed, Caen stone coffin inside the tomb. When the lid was taken off, a vision from the England of 1205 was revealed, a time when wolves ran wild and the cathedral was topped by a large golden angel. Walter's skeleton lay in his green silk Archbishop's robes, colourfully embroidered with gold thread. Underneath, the remains of a penitential hair shirt were visible. He wore silk leggings, and his brown suede boots lay in the coffin, in fine condition. His silk 'altar shoes' bore a gold ring at their tip, containing a garnet, and were decorated on the sides with a bird-headed monster. A plain yellow silk mitre was still on his head. A silver chalice, the only one known from so early in England, stood next to him, discoloured by the wine which had been left in it. A 5ft (1.5m) cedar-wood crozier lay across his body. So far, all very Christian. But the silver crozier head bore three images: a rampant horse, Persephone, and a pagan river god. A stole was decorated with profuse images, including a swastika, the ancient Indian symbol of good fortune which Hitler filched.

The ring was even stranger. Still on the skeletal hand, it was gold, of Middle Eastern origin and has been dated to

300 years after Christ. It bore the word 'XNUPHIC'; still nobody knows what it means. The jewel on it was a carved, erect serpent, with rays of light emanating from its head.

Some academics think that this ring is from the Gnostics, an early sect of Christians who are said to have preserved Jesus' mysticism. Was it a gift from Saladin himself? Some writers think so. Whoever gave it to Walter, it is, like the rest of his tomb contents, a refreshing vision of human spirituality in 1205. If you visit the tomb, you can revisit the age-old controversy about one of the four heads carved on it. With its strange headgear and un-Western face, is it Saladin himself?

TWO POETS AND A
BUTTERFLY

1905

Edward Thomas was a much-loved nature poet who became
famous as a war poet, dying at Arras in 1917. He survived
the main battle, but, as he lit a celebratory pipe, a concussion
wave from a shell killed him, aged 39. 'Adlestrop', the eve-
of-war poem about an unscheduled summer train stop, is
his masterpiece. Ted Hughes called him 'the father of us
all'. A lover of intimate country, he settled from 1905 near
Sevenoaks in Kent. There he heard about one of the
strangest characters in all of literature. W.H. Davies,
perhaps because he was a sea-captain's grandson, spent
most of his life as a compulsive hobo. Only when he mangled
his foot jumping a Canadian freight train did he slow down.
He ended up in various London tramps' hostels, often
sleeping on the streets but always writing. Although his
plain, unvarnished poems and fiction had a few reviews –
Bernard Shaw noticed them favourably – he could not live
by them. Until, that is, Edward Thomas rescued him from
the doss-house. He lent Davies a tiny cottage near him in
Kent. As Thomas's wife Helen recorded in her memoirs,
they befriended Davies, encouraged his writing and
even paid the local wheelwright to carve him a better
wooden leg.

  As an uneducated vagrant for much of his life, Davies'
confidence was not high and one day he was toiling
fruitlessly over a poem in his little Kent garden. It was a

summer morning. Suddenly, a butterfly settled on his pencil and he felt some sort of spiritual awakening. Davies' friend Richard Church recalled in 1948: 'He was never weary of mentioning that incident. The mystic in him gave it a tremendous significance.' The butterfly seemed to tell him to emerge, butterfly-like, into his full potential. Sure enough, Davies' *Autobiography of a Super-Tramp*, written at the Kent cottage, remains a much-read classic and *Young Emma*, the frank story of his love life, which lay in a bank vault until 1979, is a posthumous success. And, although kindly Edward Thomas has a plaque in Westminster Abbey for his fine work, Davies managed to write a poem which consoles millions of people. It begins:

What is this life if, full of care
We have no time to stand and stare
No time to stand beneath the boughs
And stare as long as sheep or cows.

THE ISLE OF SHEPPEY: WHERE LEONARDO'S DREAM CAME TRUE

1909

Mercury, Icarus, the Archangel Gabriel, Leonardo da Vinci. They all dreamed of flying.

But where in Kent did all those dreams become reality? On the humble Isle of Sheppey, 'the cradle of aviation', that's where.

What is it about Kent and flight? It seems that the crazy Kentish inventor played by Dick Van Dyke in *Chitty Chitty Bang Bang* was based on reality. Certainly the author of that story, Ian Fleming, knew his Kent eccentrics well. There are two extraordinary Kentish preludes to Sheppey's golden era.

First, at Bexley. Here Hiram Maxim suffered an attack of guilt. Having invented and mass-produced the Maxim machine-gun – later to become a mass killer in the Great War – he wanted to invent something more beneficial. Flushed with all his machine-gun profits, money was no object, so Victorian Bexley saw, in 1894, the astonishing trials of Maxim's giant steam-driven aeroplane, 140ft (42.7m) long, with a 125ft (38.1m) wingspan. This folly makes most other British nutty ideas, such as the Sinclair C5, look sensible. Even the propellers were 18ft (5.5m) long. But, in front of a thoroughly spooked Kent crowd, the monster flew 600ft (183m).

Curiously, this pioneer flight is overshadowed by the Wright Brothers' later 622ft (190m) flight at Kitty Hawk in the USA, largely because Maxim impatiently scrapped the project. He deserted aviation as a dead end, and moved on to working on a pine-vapour asthma inhaler. Probably the whole aeroplane scheme was an Oedipal response to his late father, who had tried to pioneer an even more insane idea called 'the helicopter'.

The second little-known Kent flight pioneer was Percy Pilcher. In his garden shed at Eynsford near Sevenoaks in 1896, he built a bamboo glider. It worked, and he sailed over the local hills regularly. In 2003, the BBC paid for a powered aeroplane to be built using Pilcher's little-known 1899 plans. It flew. Further, in fact, than the Wright Brothers' famous Kitty Hawk flight. I hope the spirit of poor Percy, who crash-landed and died before he could build his invention, was looking down from heaven with a smile.

Back to Sheppey. Being flat and largely uninhabited, it was an ideal site, in 1909, for the Short brothers to build the first aircraft factory in the world. Their workshop, under two railway arches in Battersea, had become too cramped. Next to the new factory was the world's first aerodrome, although, as an early advertisement proclaims, the word had yet to be invented and so it was charmingly known as 'Sheppey Flying Grounds'. Here it was that Pilots Licence Number One was issued, in 1910, to Claude Moore-Brabazon. Pioneer aviator and 'godfather of aviation' Frank McClean helped Shorts to buy the land on Sheppey, but he was aware that flying remained mysterious to 'the man on the Clapham omnibus'. His madcap solution, to fly solo, aged 36, from Sheppey, up the Thames and *through* Tower Bridge, was a masterstroke, and featured on most front pages around the world.

McClean had offered land to the Government for a military flying base, but only when a far-seeing young First Lord of the Admiralty, Winston Churchill, saw the proposal did anything happen. Churchill ordered the establishment of the first-ever 'Naval Air Station', on the Isle of Sheppey in 1911. In old age, a local farm-boy recalled the fliers, those magnificent men in their flying machines: 'Nobody ever thought they would get off the ground. It was as if people had attached wings to their arms and said they were going to fly to the moon.'

This tale ends with the gravelly purr of a Rolls-Royce motor car, bumping over Sheppey's poor roads to the Shorts aircraft factory. Inside are two young celebrity visitors from America, the Wright brothers. They purchased six of Shorts' planes. They knew, although history has forgotten, that Kent was where Leonardo's dream came true.

DR CRIPPEN, CAUGHT BY THE POST OFFICE

1910

Up until the 1980s, the Post Office ran its official Morse Code exams from a house in Rumsfield Road, Broadstairs. This was the address of North Foreland Radio, a station dedicated to helping shipping in distress in the North Sea and English Channel. The North Foreland is uniquely positioned to oversee the world's busiest shipping lanes, hence also the North Foreland Lighthouse, Britain's oldest. North Foreland Radio (NFR) was set up by the shipping insurers Lloyd's of London in 1901. They had an obvious commercial interest in minimising shipwrecks. In 1909, the Post Office took over the station and, using Morse Code and telegraphy, 'NFR' protected shipping until the onset of satellites and mobile phones. It was finally closed in 1991.

For 90 years, this little-known station saved hundreds of lives. The Dunkirk evacuation was one of its busiest times, and it has a place in pop music history as the station which received the final distress call from Radio Caroline. The pirate radio station was then based on the ship the *Ross Revenge*, which had run aground in a storm on the treacherous Goodwin Sands, off Deal.

NFR, revered by radio buffs, was a quintessentially decent, unshowy institution. Photographs show bespectacled boffins twiddling knobs on huge Bakelite machines in what looks like a suburban semi. It has emerged that NFR was in regular contact with its German equivalent, the equally long-established Norddeich Radio. Together they informed each other of ships in distress, quietly continuing this life-saving co-operation during two World Wars.

In 1910, when Dr Crippen first reported the disappearance of his wife from their house in Holloway, north London, nobody doubted the sincerity of this impeccably dressed American doctor. He hoped that the clever murder of his wife, and the destruction of her body, would never be suspected. When Chief Inspector Walter Dew of Scotland Yard searched his house, Crippen panicked and, with his mistress, took a ship to Canada.

This sudden flight alerted the police to Crippen's guilty conscience, so they returned to search the empty house inch by inch. Human remains were found: Crippen had poisoned his wife. It all seemed too late: the murderer was by now on the high seas.

Step forward the boffins of NFR. The sharp-eyed captain of Crippen's ship, Henry Kendall, recognised the shifty doctor from newspaper reports. Kendall was out of range of all wireless contact except for NFR, who took his message and relayed it to Scotland Yard. Inspector Dew took a faster ship to Canada, and arrested Crippen on arrival with the words: 'Good morning, Dr Crippen, do you know me? I'm Inspector Dew.'

Crippen replied, 'Thank God it's over. I couldn't stand it any longer,' and held out his wrists for handcuffs. He was hanged in Pentonville Prison. His lover was acquitted.

The tale of North Foreland Radio is well worth the telling, especially as it is so little known, and now the radio station site is covered by a large Asda supermarket.

KENT'S STRANGEST
MARRIAGE (SO FAR)

1913–62

Vita Sackville-West was unlikely to lead a conventional love life. She came from an impossibly unusual and glamorous family. Her mother was the illegitimate child of Pepita Duran, a Spanish dancer. Pepita was the mistress of Vita's grandfather, Lionel Sackville, British ambassador to the USA and lord of Knole House near Sevenoaks. Knole is one of England's oldest and largest houses. They call it a calendar house, because it is said to have seven courtyards, 52 staircases and 365 rooms. It has such rambling complexity that valuable treasures are still being found in obscure attics and wings. Growing up there, the young Vita confessed to 'involuntary pauses to think out the best route from one room to another'.

Pepita was the illegitimate daughter of a gypsy, who was a circus acrobat, and a Spanish duke, who was descended from Lucrezia Borgia. But this was in part a typical, lovable family myth. The 'duke' was just a Malaga barber, which could explain why Vita's son Nigel Nicolson called his mother 'at times pure undiluted peasant'. Pepita lived in various European houses under assumed names. In this improbable wandering household, Lionel, pillar of the aristocracy and of the Foreign Office, fathered five children. To add to the love-drama, Pepita had left her own husband to be with Lionel. Her magnetism was such that anyone who met her commented upon it: when she was accompanying

Lionel in Washington once, the President of the United States proposed to her.

Young Vita, as the historian of Knole, knew that over the centuries the Sackvilles had usually loved who they wished, when they wished. John Sackville, the 3rd Duke of Dorset (1745–99), was not atypical. He had three mistresses, the great love of his life being the third, Giovanna Zanerini, an Italian ballet dancer. Today at Knole, amid the pictures of stuffy nobles, Zanerini's scantily clad portrait is startlingly sensual.

When Vita herself fell in love with a brilliant diplomat, Harold Nicolson, they set up home in Kent, at Sissinghurst, where Vita designed the unconventional and much-visited garden. Her love life was as individual as her horticultural philosophy. Both she and Harold were bisexual and, although they loved each other deeply until death, they both took lovers of both sexes. After Vita's death in 1962, their son Nigel Nicolson was reading through her papers when he came across, in her tower study, a locked Gladstone bag. Having no key, he cut the leather from around the lock to open it. The large soft-backed notebook inside began with some attempts at short stories, but, on page 6, began an 80-page autobiographical confession. Written at 28, it detailed her obsessive love for Violet Trefusis.

In 1973, Nigel Nicolson wrote a candid book about his parents, *Portrait of a Marriage*. The book's message is that, if honesty rules, marriage can survive anything. Vita and Harold 'married for love … and each gave the other full liberty without enquiry or reproach'. With each other they had 'permanent and undiluted happiness'. The marriage, Nigel thought, was the harbour, the affairs mere 'ports-of-call'. Both Vita and Harold suffered terribly for their ideal of 'open marriage', but the steady stream of books about them shows that Kent's strangest marriage, in its sheer courage, strikes a chord among later generations. Vita knew that, one day in a less prudish future, the Gladstone bag would be prised open.

THE THANK-YOU PAINTING

1916

There are several instances of nations saying 'thank you' to Britain for its part in a World War. The King of Norway sends us the Trafalgar Square Christmas tree every year. The Dutch have renamed Arnhem bridge the John Frost Bridge or 'John Frostbrug', after its heroic defender, Johnnie Frost. These gestures are a pleasant counterbalance to the less savoury memories we have left in some parts of the world.

Although it was sadly neglected for years in the musty Town Hall, Folkestone is home to a beautiful 'thank you' gesture. During the Great War, over 60,000 Belgian refugees came to the town. The people of Folkestone gave them warm hospitality. It is evidence of the success of the Mayor's Refugee Committee that over 15,000 stayed on in the town. Belgian citizen Fredo Franzoni was one of them. A painter of large civic commissions in Charleroi, he had witnessed the dreadful massacre in that town, and so fled with his wife and two children to Folkestone.

In 1916, he presented the Town Hall with his atmospheric picture, *The Landing of the Belgian Refugees*. He had worked on it solidly for four months. With a misty Folkestone Harbour in the background, wan and exhausted refugees ascend from boats to a quayside reception committee of Folkestone residents. It is clear from a contemporary press report that Franzoni painted his own wife and children among the weary crowd.

The painting suffered over the years; the whole canvas sagged off its wooden frame, rumpling badly. In poor atmospheric conditions, sections of the paint cracked and 'cupped' (formed little concave discs). Other parts were simply dented. In 1970, two thick coats of cheap varnish were slapped on, unevenly: this coating quickly yellowed. In 2011, Kent County Council commissioned Julie Crick to restore the work. She demanded a large, insulated but unheated room in which to work on the picture on a sterilised table. This was provided, appropriately, by the Grand Hotel. King Albert of Belgium had stayed there in the war when he attended the painting's unveiling ceremony. Surprisingly, one of Crick's first actions was to leave the painting in this new atmosphere, so that the canvas could, as she put it, 'relax and lose its dents ... linen has this quality to recover'. Then she cleaned the painting, applied a non-yellowing, removable protective varnish and restretched the whole picture. Subtle repairs were performed using fine Japanese tissue and a non-invasive glue made from fish. With a virulent solvent, decades of grime were removed from the gilt frame.

The public reaction to the restoration of this painting was an amazing part of the whole story; residents of all ages came in their hundreds to watch Crick at work. Part of that 1916 spirit of compassion for the Belgians was reborn. The painting is now a cherished exhibit in a climate-controlled room at the Folkestone Museum.

CITIZEN KANE
IN THANET
1917

Alfred Harmsworth's background was unpromising. His father drank the family into poverty and, when Alfred fathered a child by a local maid, his mother kicked him out to live in a bedsit: this was 1882. University was not an option for the lowly educated lad. Instead, he became a newspaper reporter. As a self-made man, Alfred warmed to the approach of George Newnes, a pioneer populariser who founded *Tit-Bits* magazine, an early version of *Hello*. Newnes also strove to educate the masses in easily accessible magazines and books. Harmsworth's own magazine empire soon eclipsed Newnes', and he once described his philosophy of journalism as 'less British Museum and more life'.

When Alfred moved from magazines into newspapers, he was unstoppable. As he embraced new technology, hand compositors were sacked, and news was fresher, quicker and more accessible. He knew that the working middle classes did not have time to plough through the heavy broadsheet papers and so, in a garden study of his Broadstairs mansion in 1896, he designed a new paper, the *Daily Mail*. He went on to dream up the *Daily Mirror* in 1903, then bought the *Observer* and *The Times*. Wanting to give people a gossipy version of the latter for the weekend, he founded the *Sunday Times*. His power was astonishing: Prime Minister Lloyd George even showed him a budget speech in draft.

He loved Broadstairs, so when he was ennobled he chose the title Baron Northcliffe of Thanet. His whereabouts were well known, and so were his anti-German views. When the Great War came, he claimed to have been predicting German aggression since 1897, and the *Mail* ran lurid German atrocity stories: torturing our lads, bayoneting babies, etc. Lloyd George appointed him his Director of Propaganda. Perhaps understandably, in 1917, a German battleship sailed quietly into position off Broadstairs and tried to shell Harmsworth's seaside mansion. They missed, and a shell-hole in a house nearby was converted, with English pragmatism, into a pretty circular window, which can still be seen.

Harmsworth was no evil monster like *Citizen Kane*, but he did have a Kane-like emptiness at his heart. Although the *Mail* upheld family values and middle-class decency, and although he issued the cosy *Children's Encyclopaedia*, edited by avuncular Arthur Mee, Harmsworth's love life was all over the place. His grandmother raised his first child – the maid's – while he went on to marry a woman by whom he had no children. By a mistress, Kathleen, he had six children, but he relinquished her for Louise, his secretary. She was in turn replaced by a lengthy liaison with Betty, a baroness. The Broadstairs mansion, a modern Xanadu, did not echo with the laughter of his children. They rarely visited, although it had 11 bedrooms, five bathrooms and a pond with an alligator. Very much in the style of Orson Welles' *Citizen Kane*, Harmsworth's last wish was to be buried with his mother.

TWO TIMESLIPS
1920, 1996

Timeslips: utter nonsense or perfectly sound quantum physics? It was in 1927 that J.W. Dunne published *An Experiment with Time*. A down-to-earth aeronautical engineer who inspired the Wright brothers, Dunne was intrigued by his numerous precognitive dreams. He theorised that we only see time as linear – 'one thing after another' – with our conscious mind. In reality, past, present and future are all intermingled. Dunne has had a small following over the years but, within the last few years, physicists have started to sound just like him.

Professor of Astrophysics Brian Greene, author of *The Fabric of the Cosmos* (2004), like most of his colleagues, asserts: 'Time does not flow, as all time exists simultaneously at the same time.' As if this isn't mentally challenging enough, Greene cheerfully goes on to explain how both parallel universes and time travel are not just permitted by the laws of quantum physics: those laws positively demand those phenomena.

Despite this sound scientific background, I would hesitate to include two timeslip experiences in this book if it were not for the individuals who recounted them: Joseph Conrad's highly sensible wife Jessie and distinguished veteran novelist Russell Hoban.

In about 1920, Conrad and his wife were staying with friends at Bilsington Priory near Ashford. A medieval foundation of the Black Friars, it is still a fine atmospheric building, now a wedding venue, set in acres of mature parkland. Jessie was alone:

> Suddenly I heard a terrified whimper from my dog. As I gazed at the opposite wall, which seemed to dissolve before my eyes, the room became filled with a choking dust and through the haze I saw a long procession of habited monks. Slowly they passed along a hidden flight of steps, their wooden pattens [shoes] sounding in ghostly rhythm as they climbed. The return of the farmer's wife with a lamp dispelled the vision of whatever it was I saw. Yet she verified it for she said: 'Oh yes, we can tell the time by the monks' footsteps, six o'clock every evening.' The time was exactly six o'clock.[1]

And Russell Hoban, after a talk at my Canterbury bookshop in 1996, told me of a recent walk on the Wye Downs. This dramatic area, a nature reserve, has fine views across Kent and Romney Marsh. Because of its commanding position it has long been of strategic importance. Although Hoban did not know it, a Roman camp was there to guard the adjacent crossing-point of the River Stour. During his walk, a horde of tribesmen, woad-painted and armed, rushed up across the shoulder of the hill and disappeared, running into the large depression known as the Devil's Kneading Trough. He naturally assumed that this could all be explained by a re-enactment group or a film being made. However, enquiries in the village and of other walkers discounted these options and Hoban is convinced that he experienced a timeslip.

The Kent countryside has an historic role in time travel matters. Not only was an early *Doctor Who* episode filmed at Dungeness (an episode treasured by geeks as the one

---

1. Quoted in *Ghosts of Kent* (Meresbrough, Rainham, 1985), p.13

where *Doctor Who* girl Jo Grant shows her purple knickers), but also H.G. Wells, friend of J.W. Dunne, was on a country walk in the Weald when the whole plot of his masterpiece *The Time Machine* came to him.

HOW T.S. ELIOT FOUND INSPIRATION IN A MARGATE HUT

1921

T.S. Eliot's *The Wasteland* is one of the greatest poems in the English language. The official academic interpretation is that it reflects a national psyche shattered by the Great War; however, in a diary entry late in his life, Eliot reflected that the poem reflected the desolate landscape of his marriage. But for a Margate shed it might never have been written.

Eliot was a troubled soul, curmudgeonly and perverse. His most notoriously eccentric act was to leave his wife in a mental asylum for 14 years, until she died, without visiting her once.

A brilliant American student, Sanskrit scholar and critic, he had a degree from Harvard but once wrote to a friend, 'I hate university towns and university people.' Although he was encouraged to do a PhD, he ended up working in a London bank, becoming, in Dorothy Parker's words, 'so straight that he wore a five-piece suit'. In 1921, according to the bank's personnel records, he took three months off with 'a nervous breakdown'. He recuperated in East Kent, at Cliftonville's Albermarle Hotel. Cliftonville was the socially acceptable resort adjacent to tacky, working-class, kiss-me-quick, cockney-infested Margate. Paradoxically, it was a seaside hut, 'Nayland Rocks Hut', overlooking Margate sands where Eliot found peace and inspiration, about as far from a university atmosphere as could be imagined. He visited it daily, stopped reading anything and there poured out most of *The Wasteland*: 'On Margate sands I can connect nothing with nothing.'

There is another Kent reference: the famous first line, 'April is the cruellest month', satirises *The Canterbury Tales* jaunty April opening, 'When April with his showers sweet'. Chaucer's pilgrims begin their journey to East Kent bursting with optimism, but Eliot, in *The Wasteland,* was describing his own much darker, inner pilgrimage.

East Kent seems to be good for blocked writers. A costive, unconfident John Keats visited Canterbury and found it 'set him going [as a poet] like a billiard ball'. And Virginia Woolf always loved the city for helping her out of a major depressive trough.

What happened to the humble Victorian beach shelter where the twentieth century's greatest poem was forged? After decades of vandalism, graffiti and storm damage, in 2009 it became a Grade II listed building, thanks to a campaign led by Alan Bennett and poet laureate Andrew Motion. It is now looked after by English Heritage.

CHARTWELL:
THE BATTLE CHURCHILL
NEARLY LOST
1922–64

Winston Churchill's Kent home is a jewel in the National Trust's crown, a shrine where you feel the presence of 'Winnie' at every turn.

But his almost obsessive battle to keep the house cost him dearly. It is a seldom-told tale, but strangely comforting to know that this heroic figure struggled, as we all do, to reconcile dream and reality. He fell in love with the hill-top house, with its idyllic views over the Weald, in 1922, and lived there for 42 years. With his wife Clementine he shared a fine upstairs bedroom, which he called their 'aerial bower'. At Chartwell, he did most of his writing, those famous war histories and autobiographical reflections which earned him the Nobel Prize for Literature ('£12,100 tax-free, not bad!' he enthused to Clemmie). There he painted happily for hours and did his therapeutic bricklaying. Architectural critics think the house a mess, 'odd, undecided, suburban' (Pevsner), but Winston loved it, tinkering endlessly with little extensions and garden improvements. In 1926, a visiting Cabinet minister was taken on a long tour, failing miserably to get the conversation onto politics: 'He seems a good deal more interested in his ponds than anything in the world.' He always slept like a baby but once, at Chartwell in 1938, he was awake all night, aware of the inevitability of war. In a famous sentence, he recorded the dawn: 'I watched the daylight slowly creep in through the windows and saw before my mental gaze the vision of Death.' Later, on one of the blackest days of the war, with Crete lost, the magnificent HMS *Hood* sunk and Rommel advancing apace in North Africa, Winston simply left London for a day and wandered alone in Chartwell's garden. Chartwell was his solace, a key defence against the lurking depression he called his 'black dog'. Many depressives relish a big, unfeasible project – it's their glory and sometimes their downfall.

He could never really afford it. Clemmie confided to her daughter that the one time in 57 years that Winston deceived her was over how expensive Chartwell would be to keep. Even after he lost, in today's money, half a million pounds in the New York Crash, he ploughed on with Chartwell's upkeep and improvements, designed with society architect Philip Tilden. Often, the house was mostly dustsheeted while the Churchills occupied a corner. For a while, they had to occupy nearby Wellstreet Cottage, which had been intended for a butler. (Interestingly, the family loved its cosiness.) In 1937, not long before he took up the struggle against the Third Reich, he admitted domestic defeat to Clemmie, and reluctantly resolved to sell: 'No good offer can be refused, having regard to the fact that all children are almost flown and my life is probably in its closing decade.' (He would live for nearly 30 years more.) Knight Frank and Rutley offered it for sale in 1938: '19 bedrooms, 8 bathrooms, occupying a magnificent position on the slopes of the Kentish hills'. Then, a mysterious South African millionaire admirer, Sir Henry Strakosch, financed Churchill so that he could stay in his beloved house. Strakosch demanded no favours for this, indeed he never even visited the house. In his will he left Churchill a further £20,000. This benefactor tided Winston over until, in 1945, the National Trust procured the house in such a way that Churchill could continue to live in it. He had kept his dreamy retreat, to live in all his days – but only by the kindness of a stranger.

A KENT ROMANOV?

1923

In 1918, the Bolsheviks assassinated the Tsar and his family at Ekaterinburg in Russia. Like Elvis, Romanovs have been spotted ever since all over the world. Recent DNA matching of surviving bones from the site, using the DNA of the Duke of Edinburgh – a relative of the Romanovs – seemed to prove that all of the Tsar's family were indeed killed. However, Romanov-watchers have not given up. They point out that, with all the remains burned, DNA can only say 'Here lay a Romanov', rather than exactly which Romanovs. And of course, they say, no Russian Government wants to deal with a Romanov rediscovered, especially now that the Russian Church has made the whole clan into saints.

One of the craziest claims of all is that the Grand Duchess Tatiana, daughter of Tsar Nicholas, lived and died in humble Lydd, on the flatlands near Ashford (her sister, Anastasia, is also the subject of many survival theories). An officer in the Tank Regiment, Owen Tudor, met 'Larissa' in Constantinople after the Great War. She was a dancer, and little is known of her early life. They married in 1923 and Owen and Larissa Tudor lived in a humble cottage on the green in Lydd. Larissa died in 1926, of tuberculosis. Perhaps the very remoteness of Lydd was ideal for a Romanov, say the conspiracy theorists. Other absurd speculation includes a mystery restoration of her grave, apparently by an anonymous Russian.

Six hard facts nevertheless remain unchallenged.

1. Colonel Meinertzhagen, a senior British spy held in awe by Lawrence of Arabia, described a rescue mission to Ekaterinburg. In his diaries he says the mission failed, but that one Romanov girl was grabbed and 'literally thrown into our plane'. The colonel was a self-advertising character, but, for what it's worth, my father knew him and was deeply impressed by what Lawrence called 'that savage brain'.

2. Larissa Tudor had different dates of birth on her marriage certificate, death certificate and tombstone. Significant?

3. Espionage historian Michael Occleshaw interviewed an old lady in Lydd who used to chat to Larissa over her garden wall, and, when shown a photograph of Tatiana, said it was Larissa. Other aged Lydd residents picked out Tatiana's image from those of random women of the period, recalling her distinctive auburn hair, tinged with red.

4. Despite her humble home, when Larissa died, she left a large inheritance.

5. On her tombstone, erected by her husband, she is called Larissa Feodorovna Tudor. Feodorovna was the Grand Duchess' surname.

6. When Owen Tudor remarried after Larissa's death, one of the guests was Lady Mary Cambridge, a close relative of both the British and Russian royal families.

It might all be nonsense but, like visiting a church even if you don't believe in God, it makes a wistful trip to Lydd worthwhile.

WHERE IS THE REAL CHITTY CHITTY BANG BANG?

1923

Every few years, newspapers carry reports of the sale of 'the original Chitty Chitty Bang Bang'. They are all nonsense. Six versions of 'Chitty' were made for the 1968 film. These 'magical flying cars' really worked, and it is these that periodically come up for sale. The May 2011 auction sale of 'the original Chitty', for £1.2 million, was a typical example.

The tale of the real Chitty is buried in the heart of the countryside near Canterbury. There, in 1910, a Polish playboy inherited a great house, Higham Park, in Bridge, still in private hands today. He was Count Zborowski, and at just 16 years old he inherited Higham Park, £11 million and 7 acres (2.8ha) of Manhattan. Wildness ensued, and parties at Higham were as grand as the old days when Mozart and Gainsborough had visited. The Count's father had died in a motor-racing crash but young Zborowski, undeterred, took to racing zestfully, driving early Aston Martins and Bugattis. Sadly, Zborowski would himself die in a racing accident in 1924, aged only 29.

The young Count loved to experiment. He tested explosives by blowing up statues at Higham – pieces went as far as half a mile (0.8km) away. He made a narrow-gauge railway track around the estate, commissioning special small steam locomotives to run on it. This was so much fun that, with a racing chum called Captain Howey, he planned the Romney, Hythe and Dymchurch Light Railway.

It has delighted millions and still carries children to school. But his pièce de résistance was when he put an aeroplane engine into a car, and Chitty Chitty Bang Bang was born. Ian Fleming was a boy in the crowd watching this roaring monster race at Brooklands racetrack. He went on to write the book *Chitty Chitty Bang Bang*, which was made into a film script by Roald Dahl. The eccentric inventor Caractacus Potts, played by Dick Van Dyke in the film, was partly inspired by Count Zborowski.

Chitty was therefore a real car, but what happened to it? The answer is not in any book, or anywhere on the internet. It is on the wall of the Plough and Harrow pub in Bridge, near Canterbury. This is the humblest and cosiest of the village's three pubs. Friendly and slightly raucous, it is a place of lively darts tournaments, local kids climbing up onto bar stools and sun-tanned old farmers. There are no fondue nights, no swirly carpets and no air fresheners in the lavatories.

A series of captioned black-and-white photographs, evidently placed there by estate workers, follows the history of Chitty. Here it is explained that Count Zborowski loved the car so much that he could not bear to think of other people driving it. He ordered it to be buried at a secret location in the grounds of Higham Park. Perhaps some future TV archaeology programme will discover the car which made millions of children happy, buried by the childless man who never really grew up.

THE SECRET OF BILLY BUNTER

1926–61

Frank Richards' *Billy Bunter* stories were astonishingly popular throughout most of the twentieth century. Bunter's chums, sporty Harry Wharton, thoroughly good Bob Cherry and ever-courteous Sir Hurree Jamset Ram, lived in a cosily riotous boarding-school world of tuck, pranks and friendship. They had their own obscure public-school jargon, and at intervals the famous cry went up, as the form master approached, 'Crikey, here comes Quelch!' Bunter, a snobbish, babbling, treacherous glutton, is a superb creation. Curiously, we like him. Perhaps, as George Orwell – a big Bunter fan – suggested, he's a young Falstaff, lovably larger-than-life for all his faults, patently vulnerable in all his scheming.

Richards lived, from 1926 until his death in 1961, in Rose Lawn, a humble suburban Broadstairs villa, with his housekeeper. A recluse, he allowed few visitors and seldom ventured into town. He even ordered shopping by phone. Ingeniously, he avoided journeying to the bank by posting a cheque to them and getting them to post him cash. As a schoolboy in the 1950s, an awed Frank Muir used to spot him in Rose Lawn's garden, with a cat and his trademark skull-cap, pipe and the purple dressing-gown which he wore over his clothes. Over the years, on his trusty Remington typewriter, he bashed out 80 million words about not just Greyfriars – Bunter's school – but 100 other invented schools. He used over 20 pseudonyms. *The Guinness Book of Records* cited him as the world's most prolific author.

His achievement was to enshrine the joys of boarding-school life in the British imagination, especially after the long-running Bunter TV series and the many Bunter theatre plays. But Bunter's secret is that his creator had never been to boarding school. This explains why his autobiography starts at the age of 17. Like his vivid tales of China and British Columbia, which he never visited, he imagined it all. Yet thousands of children wrote to Bunter and chums as if they were real. The GPO had to provide a special forwarding service, as it did for all the letters to Sherlock Holmes and Father Christmas. Richards – real name Charles Hamilton – was born in a smoke-blackened Ealing terrace, in a tiny one-up one-down house, one of the eight children of an alcoholic journalist who died at 45, when poor Richards was seven. The author grew up to endure a seldom-mentioned passionate love affair, then a phase of gambling addiction, before he got religion and set about furiously writing himself out of debt, and away from his humble origins. So ends the tale of a little-known Kent writer who pleased millions of children simply because, as he freely admitted, he 'never really stopped being a boy'. He probably led his reclusive existence in part because he was not the boarding-school product which readers would expect him to be. By the time of his death, he had acquired such obscurity that his housekeeper called a local reporter with the news and asked, 'Do you think anyone will be interested?'

GYPSY ROYALTY

1933

In 1933, Arthur Mee was touring Kent, researching his series of guide books, *The King's England*. Mee was a *Daily Mail* journalist who lived in a Kent mansion, over which flew, at all times, a large Union Jack. An Empire-loving English nationalist, he stumbled upon an occasion in Farnborough, North Kent, which was not exactly his 'cup of tea'. Here, in 1933, the Gypsy Queen, Urania Lee, was buried, and Mee saw 'her royal caravan, still parked in the lane'. Mee was lucky: he was present at one of the great moments in Romany history.

Gypsy history is largely oral; they make music, dance, paint and know horses, but their culture remains mysterious, because they are wanderers, excluded and persecuted. Even this persecution has scarcely been written about in books, in contrast to the mountains of Holocaust literature in existence. Hitler included gypsies in his 'Final Solution', and recent research indicates that over 1.5 million were killed by the Nazis. In 2010, the French Government used armed police to conduct a compulsory mass deportation of gypsies to Romania. Although Romania is one of their homelands, research into their strange language indicates that they originate in India.

In Britain, for many centuries, the two great gypsy clans were the Boswells and Lees. When Gypsy King Levi Boswell married Urania Lee, they set up base camp at

Farnborough and became King and Queen of our gypsies. Levi kept hundreds of thoroughbred horses on the site of modern-day Farnborough Hospital and this merited many visits from the British aristocracy, who usually then had their fortunes told by Urania. Levi's 1924 Farnborough funeral, reported in *The Times*, was extraordinary: over a thousand gypsies from all over Britain saw six black horses pull Levi's funeral carriage. Urania attended on crutches; an inveterate and skilled horse-breaker, she was recovering from one of her many accidents.

A *Kentish Times* reporter attended Urania's 1933 lying in state, and saw gypsies from far and wide file into her tiny room, amid gleaming polished brass and bunches of wild flowers. He also reported a conversation with her nephew, who had always refused to have her tell his fortune; she was so accurate that he preferred blissful ignorance. As an example, he related that Urania correctly predicted her own death. After the cries of the 'Death Bird' were heard at night, she told relatives that 'tomorrow at six or seven in the morning I'll say goodbye'. She died at 6.45a.m. She was 82 years old.

Kent's gypsy royalty have a little-known legacy. In the 1900s, Levi Boswell started a sideline in selling donkey rides to children, outside the park gates at Greenwich; he would take the donkeys back to Farnborough each night. The donkey rides continue to this day at the same spot.

'GOD, WHAT A FAMILY' – EVELYN WAUGH

1934

Waugh wrote this quote with mingled admiration and love for the Lygon family. Their elegant, straight-laced, but complicated and close-knit family directly inspired his greatest book, and one of the greatest ever written, *Brideshead Revisited*. Like Lord Marchmain in the book – so vividly played by Laurence Olivier in the television series – William Lygon, Earl Beauchamp, was driven to exile in Europe by scandal.

The Lygons were of another age. They migrated between their three houses, a town house in Belgravia, the ancestral seat in Worcestershire, Madresfield, and Walmer Castle, near Deal, East Kent. William, the Earl, occupied the castle as Lord Warden of the Cinque Ports (1913–34). Twenty-five staff, including liveried footmen in breeches and powdered wigs, accompanied the Lygons' frequent house moves. At dinner, the seven children – four girls and three boys – addressed their father in turn, often in French, with a footman standing behind each chair. Father was chosen to hold the Sword of State at the 1911 Coronation.

Despite all that, Lygon was a very non-traditional toff. A devoted 'hands-on' father, he played a lot with his children and was deeply loved by them in return. Late in life, Waugh was to regret that his own children did not give him Lygon-style affection: he especially remembered how Lygon children loved bringing their father cocktails in the bath and chatting away there with him. Also atypically, in politics the Earl was both active and radical. Highly valued by the Liberals, he was privately drawn to the Socialists, but 'didn't think', his daughter recalled, 'that they'd have someone like him'. A Cabinet member who frequently had the Prime Minister, Asquith, to stay at Walmer, he fought for Irish Home Rule, sexual equality and the League of Nations. A pacifist, he used his influence to argue for a negotiated end to the Great War, and to protect conscientious objectors from harassment. He was especially happy when he procured the dismissal of the Wandsworth Prison Governor who allowed the torture of 'conchies'. An early 'green', he was active in the rambling movement and in the fledgling National Trust.

Atmospheric black-and-white photographs at Walmer Castle show the family. We see the distant, overpious mother who hit her children, especially the slightly deaf daughter, and, for birthdays, only gave church candles. I have searched in vain in two recent family biographies – both by women – for the good side of Lady Beauchamp. When I came across her delight in parodying disabled children whom she saw in London, trying in vain to get her children to join in, I gave up. We also see the dashing Earl, usually in white flannels, at ease with his children.

Jealousy ended the idyll. The Earl's brother-in-law, the Duke of Westminster, although the richest man in England, was too dim to get anywhere in politics. Nor could he rival the Lygon fecundity, siring only one heir, despite four unhappy marriages and several affairs. Although the establishment closed ranks to conceal his penchant for very young girls, and tolerated his rampant anti-Semitism, as a divorcee he was banned from Court, a source of more rancour: he was especially bitter that Lygon officiated at the Coronation. But he knew Lygon's Achilles heel: he was bisexual, a source of torment when he was at school, and so the rival Duke set private detectives to follow his relative. They interviewed staff at Walmer, and discovered that he had 'relations' with servants and local fishermen. When Westminster told his sister, she filed for divorce, and when the King was informed, he reportedly replied, 'I thought men like that shot themselves.' Aristocratic sexual adventurism was rife: the toffs' Eleventh Commandment was well known: 'Thou Shalt not Get Caught'. But the newspapers had been told, and William Lygon, seventh Earl Beauchamp, had been caught. Something had to be done, especially in the light of Lygon's favoured position, so close to the throne. So in 1934 three Lords, all known to him, called on the Earl at Madresfield, unannounced. He was dozing in an armchair. They told him that, to avoid a public trial – homosexuality being illegal at that time – he would have to leave his family and Britain, for good, forthwith. Westminster wrote to him: 'Dear Bugger-in-Law, you got what you deserved'. Although shortly afterwards he attempted suicide, Lygon went on to write weekly to all his children, from his various lodgings around Europe. Amazingly, they all stayed loyal to him, and visited him on a rota system, so that he would never be without one for long. Furious at their mother's complicity in exposing their father's bisexuality, which they had suspected anyway, they rarely spoke to her again. She died, at 59, in 1936.

When his son Hugh died young, in 1936, the Earl could see no way to return for the funeral, but the Lygon beauty came to the rescue: Sibell Lygon was Lord Beaverbrook's lover, and he got the ban on the Earl's return lifted. The Earl too would die soon, in 1938, at 66.

If you visit Walmer Castle today you can see those Lygon family photos, and feel in the gardens the ghost of a family which need not have been so drastically broken apart. Although the children rarely gave interviews, Sibell, who died at 98 in 2005, was asked in old age, by a biographer, how she wanted her father portrayed. She replied, 'Just the truth; he was a very nice man and he did so care about his children.'

FOUR INCREDIBLY STRANGE ANTI-NAZI INVENTIONS

1940–45

Churchill would do anything to beat Hitler, and so no scheme was too far-fetched. You can call this English eccentricity, or lateral thinking. For instance, when my own father offered to find mines at sea by dowsing, Winston gave him an honoured place on a destroyer, to try him out. The introduction of radar rendered the ancient art of dowsing unnecessary to the war effort, however.

Kent is the scene of four incredibly strange anti-Nazi inventions. They were all sanctioned by Churchill but few of us today would have listened to their inventors for 15 minutes. It is a measure of his greatness that they all worked.

1. 'The Boche Buster'. This was a gigantic gun, mounted on a train, which took two days to travel from Yorkshire, where it had been assembled, to Kent. It was kept on the Canterbury to Folkestone line. In the event of an invasion, it could decimate an advancing German army anywhere in Kent, and it was placed on this winding branch line specifically because it thereby had the ability to point at any part of East Kent. It would fire its shell and then move on, evading the Luftwaffe. Cunningly, when not in use it hid in a long tunnel at Etchinghill. Although it could fire a shell 12 miles (19.3km), it unfortunately had a recoil force equivalent to 420 tons, so shot back about 40ft (12.2m) up the line

when fired, amid clouds of trackbed dust. An elderly local near the line has shown me the cracks in their house, caused by the Boche Buster's test firing. She said that many houses in the area sustained dramatic cracks. Churchill paid a visit to the railway gun in 1941.

2. The Bouncing Bomb. Inventor Barnes Wallis thought that he could get a spherical bomb to bounce on water, like a skimming pebble, thus evading enemy torpedo nets, and detonate against a dam wall. Wallis's experiments with golf balls in water tanks were memorably portrayed on film, with Michael Redgrave playing Wallis. Churchill authorised the idea and it was tested off Herne Bay. In 1997, that test bomb was located on the seabed and brought up: it is now in Herne Bay Museum. The Bouncing Bomb went on to break the Ruhr dams and flood part of the German industrial heartland.

3. The Maunsell Sea Forts. In 1961, father-of-two Guy Maunsell, an amateur watercolour painter, died aged 77 in quiet obscurity at Tunbridge Wells. This reclusive figure was one of Britain's unsung wartime inventors, and his creations are still very visible, far out at sea, from Herne Bay. In 1941, Churchill was concerned at the German bombing, via the Mersey, of Liverpool docks; he knew that London, the world's biggest port, was just as vulnerable to an upriver raid. Maunsell designed concrete forts, which were pre-constructed, floated out and sunk into sandbanks. From guns mounted on these lonely outposts, 22 enemy aircraft and 30 flying bombs, heading for London, were shot down. The forts were way ahead of their time, for this was decades before any open-sea oil rigs were built.

4. Sound Mirrors. These gigantic 'concrete ears' can still be seen at Dungeness and Hythe. They were designed to pick up the sound of approaching enemy aircraft, and were effective until rendered obsolete by radar, and faster planes. Ignored, ridiculed and neglected for years, in 2003 English Heritage protected them as listed buildings.

All of these four adventures in technology were supported by Churchill, a man who, as a young soldier on the Sudan Campaign, rode in the last major British cavalry charge, in 1899.

THE OLD LADY WHO TRICKED THE LUFTWAFFE

1940

During the Battle of Britain in the summer of 1940, the people of Kent watched as the RAF fought the Luftwaffe in dogfights over the Garden of England. The film *The Battle of Britain* has imprinted the drama on our imagination, with its all-star cast and Technicolor countryside. In the Jackdaw pub at Denton, near Canterbury, you can sit in the chair which 'pilot' Michael Caine occupied and imagine Susannah York at the bar with Christopher Plummer.

During the battle, many German airmen bailed out or crash-landed in Kent. Near Sevenoaks, one surrendered to an approaching bus conductor, assuming his curious uniform to represent an obscure unit of the British Army. At Shoreham, a young German pilot was so white-faced and shaken that the Home Guard bought him a double brandy in the pub before taking him to be locked up. But surely the most thoroughly British capture of a Nazi in the whole war must be the one involving an old lady who lived in a cottage near Headcorn. She spotted a Luftwaffe pilot on the run, invited him in for tea, gave him a slice of cake, then nipped into her hallway and quietly telephoned the police. She successfully kept him chatting in broken English until they arrived.

THE SPY WHO ESCAPED DOWN THE THIRTY-NINE STEPS

1940

Nobody in genteel 1930s Broadstairs suspected that a Gestapo spy was living in their midst. Dr Arthur Tester was every inch an Englishman, though born in Stuttgart, where his father had been British consul. He was apparently a pillar of the community, inhabiting an ostentatious clifftop villa near Broadstairs, just below the North Foreland Lighthouse. The house had been built by an old Raj hand, so it was called Naldera, after an Indian hill station near Simla. Tester kept the name, married and had five children. His daughter was known locally as a promising ballerina.

But the spy was a cigar-toting wide boy, a suave and sinister villain worthy of an Ian Fleming or Graham Greene novel. I strongly suspect he wore an astrakhan coat. He was an opportunist with an Arthur Daley-style entrepreneurial streak, and, having had an uncomfortable internment by the Germans in the First World War, he was more than happy to offer the Nazis his dodgy services to avoid a second incarceration. So, in wartime England, he entertained business contacts on his luxury yacht *Lucinda*, especially fascist sympathisers. One of his many companies, British Glycerine Manufacturers, had a smart head office at 14 St James' Place, London. Its title was as fake as Tester's 'Dr': its function was to transfer black-shirt sympathisers' money into fascist regimes.

Tester's London-based European Press Agency also

seemed innocent, but it fed anti-Semitic and anti-Communist 'news stories' to European newspapers. The agency was founded on a deposit of £100,000, the cheque signed by a certain Dr Goebbels. Tester even tried to set up a cinema chain to show pro-Nazi films.

One evening soon after the start of the Second World War, Kent police descended on Naldera: it was deserted and in darkness. Months before, Mrs Tester and the children had quietly fled to Nazi Europe. Tester himself had slipped away earlier that evening, to a rowing boat which took him to a German submarine. The discreet way down the cliffs is via the Thirty-nine Steps, that staircase to the beach which John Buchan saw when, living in Broadstairs, he wrote his classic spy adventure. Buchan had conceived the steps as a spy's escape route and now, 25 years after the book was published, life was imitating art.

Unfortunately for Tester, towards the end of the war, the Russians were to track him down in Romania. On a mountain car-chase, he swerved off the road, crashed and was shot dead. MI5, keen to confirm that the evil Tester was dead, persuaded the Russians, with difficulty, to exhume the body a year after his death. He was identified from the records of his Broadstairs dentist.

THE WOMAN WHO COMPLAINED ABOUT THE WAR

1940

RAF Manston, near Ramsgate, was one of the busiest airfields in Kent during the Second World War. It now houses a large wartime museum, including an original Spitfire, that legendary Battle of Britain fighter aircraft. Being on the large, flat plain of cabbage fields in Thanet, Manston was able to have a huge runway, 9,000ft (2,744m) long by 750ft (229m) wide. It was the closest airbase to Nazi-occupied Europe, a fact that could not be hidden from German reconnaissance planes (although a rival, fake, decoy airbase on Ash marshes, complete with buildings made of canvas, did fool the Germans for a while).

Naturally, the Luftwaffe hammered Manston repeatedly. The worst year was 1940. Early on 12 May, a clear spring day, an 'armada' of Luftwaffe planes headed for Manston, having first knocked out all five of the coastal radar stations which might have tracked their progress. Hangars were wrecked, all buildings were set ablaze, several Spitfires were destroyed on the ground, and the runway was left with over a hundred craters.

But the worst attack on Manston came at midday late in August, when a specially formed crack German squadron flew in low from Calais, machine-gunning and dropping bombs. Although two Messerschmitts were shot down – one from a machine-gun mounted on a jeep – Manston was now devastated, the airfield littered with unexploded bombs, seven people dead, many injured, and all communication lines cut. Worried staff at RAF Fighter Command in Maidstone, unable to contact the base, sent a lone cyclist from a nearby lookout post to find out what had happened. The base closed down, as the enemy had hoped. Fighter squadrons transferred to RAF Hornchurch in Essex. However, hearing of the plight of his key airfield, Winston Churchill visited Manston on 28 August. By firing off orders in all directions and using one of his famous and galvanising 'Action This Day' memoranda, he got the airbase up and running in an incredible 36 hours.

The station commander, Squadron-Leader George Manton, having survived all this, and with communications restored, received an indignant phone call from a local squire's wife complaining about all the recent noise. What, she demanded, was he going to do about it?

Commendably, the exhausted Manton regarded the call as a welcome piece of light relief.

FORTY YEARS OF MISPLACED GUILT, AND A MYSTERY

1941

Amy Johnson was a Hull typist who, in several ways, broke the mould of early twentieth-century womanhood. The daughter of a self-made man, a northern businessman who had 'pulled himself up by his bootstraps', Amy was a handful from early on. At 12, she was riding her father's motorbike illicitly while he was at work. When told that her passion for swimming was 'unladylike', she took up trapeze, and then cricket, at which she excelled, bowling overarm.

In the 1920s, she gained an Economics degree, when only a few, mostly aristocratic, women could consider university. She had been a twitchy undergraduate, uncomfortable with long spells of uninterrupted study. 'I have decided,' she wrote to her German boyfriend, 'that utter boredom is responsible for more crimes than wickedness.'

In 1928, she was on the top deck of a bus passing an aerodrome. This was a solution to boredom. She got off the bus and her life was changed forever. It shows how courageous, or reckless, she was that, just two years later, she flew solo to Australia, setting a new world record. An unimaginable 200,000 people greeted her return at Croydon airport, and now the tiny plane she flew hangs from the ceiling of the Science Museum in London. She became a worldwide celebrity overnight and, when she married fellow aviator Jim Mollison, they became the Richard Burton and Liz Taylor, or the Posh and Becks, of their day. Their fame was celebrated in many ways, including a ticker-tape parade when they flew to New York, and an audience with President Roosevelt. A film was made about them, and the hit song 'Amy, Wonderful Amy' seemed to say it all.

The Second World War provided ample outlet for Amy's adrenalin addiction. As an officer in the Air Transport Auxiliary Corps, she set off one day in December 1941 from Glasgow Airport, for Oxford. It was dangerous, snowy weather. Blown off course, she ditched in the Thames Estuary, just off Herne Bay. This relatively unglamorous site seems an ironically long way from the usual venues of her glamorous career. HMS *Haslemere* sped to her side as she waved and shouted from the sea. Its captain, Walter Fletcher, dived in to save her. Tragically, both died in the freezing water. The heroic Fletcher is buried on a hill overlooking the estuary, at Gillingham.

For decades, this was seen as a Kent wartime tragedy, with the weather as the villain. But in 1999 Tom Mitchell, an old soldier in his eighties, contacted his local paper with a different story. He could not contain his guilt any more: he had shot Amy down.

Sitting in his anti-aircraft battery near the sea, he had challenged the low-flying aircraft over the radio for the correct password. Twice, Johnson had failed to give the correct code. So he had sent up 16 shells, and seen the plane go down. Only the next day did he discover that Amy had died that day. His senior officers told him to keep quiet.

Poor Tom Mitchell, who had poured out his remorse at the time in confidential letters to his sister, need not have suffered those 40 years of guilt. Thanks in part to detective work by Amy's biographer Midge Gillies, an even stranger tale can be told. The *Haslemere*'s crew saw Amy in the water so clearly that at first they thought, with her fresh complexion and high voice, she was a boy. They threw her ropes but there was a heavy swell and she could not get them with her numb hands. Fletcher jumped in and held her briefly, but soon afterwards the *Haslemere*'s stern rose up and crashed on top of her. Fletcher was dragged back on to the ship, but died soon afterwards. Although everyone was reluctant to tell the family or the public about the grim detail of Amy's sad end, it is thought she was killed by the ship's propellers.

Poor old Tom's testimony is destroyed by several facts: principally, that he fired on a plane hours after Amy's death, and that Amy had no radio. So, now that Amy's death is clearer, only the mystery of 'Mr X' remains. Several people saw a man in the water with Amy, and the government still refuse to give the purpose of her mission. There is a rumour that her destination was Germany, and Herne Bay is indeed very far off-course from Oxford. Many insist that her floating pigskin bag was mistaken for 'Mr X'. Next time you visit the Science Museum, you can see Amy's bag: to me it makes an unconvincing 'man'. But neither Amy's body, nor anyone else's, was ever recovered – officially.

A MODERN SAINT'S SHRINE IN ASHFORD

1943

Even the most devoted residents admit that Ashford is known as a bit of a dump. Many of its few remaining characterful houses were demolished for a 'racetrack' ring-road. Eurostar trains were supposed to make the town prosper, but, increasingly, they don't stop there. In my Canterbury bookshop a customer once exclaimed, holding up a copy of *1000 Places to See Before You Die,* 'Oh my God, this book has got Ashford in it!' Wild-eyed with incredulity, I stumbled headlong towards the customer to look for myself. (I had misheard. The book had an entry on Auschwitz.)

But, like many outwardly unpromising towns, Ashford has its unlikely genius-association. Think of Philip Larkin in Hull, *Empire of the Sun* author J.G. Ballard in his peeling Shepperton semi, and J.D. Salinger in New Hampshire suburbia. Certain sorts of radical free-thinkers bear out the Shakespearean idea that 'to the wise man any port's a happy haven'. Philosopher and mystic Simone Weil had no bourgeois snobbery about Ashford, exclaiming with joy when she saw her room in the TB sanatorium there. All she needed was her small collection of favourite books, Plato's *Republic*, St John of the Cross and the Hindu scripture, the *Bhagavad Gita*.

The town, built around railway works and factories, was bound to appeal to her love of workers. So why is Ashford's resident genius so little known? Probably because Weil, apart from only living there in the few months before she died in 1943, was decades ahead of her time. The world is only slowly catching up with the courage of her thought. A child prodigy who knew Ancient Greek at 12, Weil defies categorisation. Philosophically, she was more Groucho Marx than Karl Marx. Groucho said, 'I'd never join a club that would have me as a member.' She subverted every creed or dogma going, insisting on interpreting them her own way, according to her extraordinary conscience. Here is the impressive list of clubs Weil could not join:

Philosophy: She attended the intellectual hothouse *École Superieure*, along with Sartre. Renowned French philosopher Albert Camus was in awe of Weil's work. Iris Murdoch ranked her with Wittgenstein and Nietzsche. But Weil hated Nietzsche, and left philosophy in disgust to work on the factory floor, doing long gruelling shifts in places such as the Renault factory.

Fascism: As early as 1932, she had visited Germany and dismissed Hitler as a 'dangerous little boy'.

Communism: She knew Trotsky well but had a blazing row with him, audible in the next house, because he thought violence was justified in a revolution.

Gaullism: She was in the French Resistance but her disgust at extreme French nationalism, and her opposition to French colonialism in North Africa, led many fellow-fighters to disown her as a traitor.

Zionism: Weil's fellow Jews were infuriated with her, because she opposed the establishment of Israel.

Roman Catholicism: Deeply connected with Catholicism,

having been transformed by a mystical experience at Assisi in 1937, she angered the Catholic clergy by insisting that organised, Pope-led Christianity was the original totalitarianism. Without Christianity's history of tormenting heretics, she argued, Nazism and the Holocaust could not have happened. She invented a personal creed, a fusion of Plato and Christianity, with influences from Hinduism and Buddhism (she learned Sanskrit and Tibetan to study those religions).

Feminism: In Paris, she snubbed the 'founding mother of feminism' Simone de Beauvoir (who admired her greatly), telling her 'the trouble with you is you've never gone hungry'.

Femininity: A noted beauty, she wore such un-feminine clothes that she was accused of cross-dressing. Famously clumsy, she smoked badly made roll-ups all her life and was usually covered in tobacco. Even aged three, she expressed a 'dislike of luxury'. Paradoxically, eroticist George Bataille loved her pallid skin and dark clothing. He called her a Don Quixote figure, forever courageously fighting for impossibly high ideals.

It is true that, unlike other philosophers, she quietly helped the poor all her life, wearing herself out in the process. She gave away much of her wages, and usually lived in slum areas, even the grimmest part of Harlem in New York, where children queued up in the evenings because she always helped them out with homework.

This brings me to the final twist in the tale, the reason that flowers are usually to be found on Weil's Ashford gravestone. For all her abrasive critique of Christianity, it has emerged that she was baptised late in life. This, combined with her asceticism and self-sacrifice, has led to some calling for her to be made a saint. Her niece, Sylvie, who looks uncannily like Simone, is often approached by devotees who touch her clothes and sometimes try to run their fingers through her hair. The reputation of the self-effacing chain-smoker who died at 34 just grows. Ashford Council named a road after her. There are three biographies, while an opera, a jazz CD and a film all try to portray this elusive crusader for the poor.

JAMES BOND, A BUS AND THE SEARCH FOR HAPPINESS

1952

James Bond experts agree that author Ian Fleming got the spy's code name from the Dover–London bus. The service ran right through the village of Bridge, near Canterbury, where Fleming often stayed. Although the bus now travels along the nearby A2, it is still the 007. And much of *Moonraker* is set in Kent, the missile plant run by evil Hugo Drax being located in the seaside village of Kingsdown, between Dover and Deal.

Fleming loved Kent. At St Margaret's Bay near Deal, he was able to quietly spend days and nights with Ann, his long-term lover, who was then married to Viscount Rothermere. After Ian and Ann's eventual marriage in 1952, they bought Noel Coward's bungalow under the cliffs there as a weekend retreat. A humble dwelling – 'This, I suppose, is how the poor live,' sneered visiting toff Duff Cooper – it nevertheless hosted many creative houseguests. Coward himself stayed, as did Evelyn Waugh, painter Lucian Freud, travel writer Patrick Leigh Fermor and critic Cyril Connolly, whose wife remembered Ian, 'tanned and thinner', Ann, 'greyer, older, happier and obviously pregnant', and that both of them were 'more lovebirdy than ever and kept putting their heads together to inspect holes in the carpet'. Charades and canasta were frequent pursuits. When the baby, Caspar, was born, Ann stayed at St Margaret's with him for long happy months. Poignantly in view of later events, photographer Cecil Beaton wrote excitedly to Greta Garbo: 'What will the child grow up to be?'

Increasingly though, there was a dark side to the Kentish idyll, uncovered in Andrew Lycett's *Ian Fleming*. Ian's horror of 'abnormality' meant that he was repelled by Ann's Caesarean scars. Intimacy lessened. Fleming was a typically Etonian parent: distant but with very set views. At St Margaret's, Caspar stayed in the nanny's quarters until some evening 'bonding time' with Daddy. As Fleming's career bloomed, he and Ann moved their retreat to Archbishop Cranmer's Tudor house, the Old Palace at Bekesbourne, near Canterbury. Ann, an earl's granddaughter, told Evelyn Waugh that the neighbours were just not up to scratch: 'neither landed nor peasantry'. Ann had tired of loving Ian, and even sadomasochism no longer spiced up their love. She had adored him to whip her and he had once written promising her 20 lashes, 'ten on each buttock'. As Ian spent more and more time with his Caribbean mistress Blanche in Jamaica, he resisted Ann visiting him there, especially with Caspar. Although Ann had her own lover, the married Labour Party leader Hugh Gaitskell, he was never as important to her as Blanche was to Ian, who immortalised his mistress as Pussy Galore in *Goldfinger*.

In 1964, the year of his death, Bond's creator lived for a while in a cottage at Pett Bottom, near Canterbury. He used the garden of his local pub, the Duck Inn, to write the last James Bond book which he would see published, *You Only Live Twice*. His favourite bench now bears a plaque. The book recalls Commander Bond's childhood 'in the quaintly named hamlet of Pett Bottom', living with a kindly aunt after his parents' death. The aunt educated Bond at home in the village, before the wrench of his departure for Eton at 12. It is generally agreed that, although Bond was based on various spies, his dashing, womanising life was a wishful version of Fleming's own life. It is poignant that just before his death he was evoking a cosseted, pre-boarding-school existence for his avatar, Bond. Fleming, a relentless smoker and over-drinker, died in Canterbury at just 56. Heartbreakingly, his only son Caspar, for whom he made up the stories which later became *Chitty Chitty Bang Bang*, committed suicide by an overdose in 1975, aged only 23. He was buried next to his father.

The Flemings, for all the tragedies, had some of their happiest times in East Kent, and James Bond's roots are here more than anywhere else.

SISSINGHURST: WHAT THE NATIONAL TRUST WON'T TELL YOU

1954

Sissinghurst Castle, near Cranbrook in West Kent, is one of the great visitor attractions of Kent. Its owner, Sir Harold Nicolson, was outwardly a pillar of the establishment. He was the diplomat who handed the declaration of war in 1914 to the German Ambassador, went on to become a Labour MP, a BBC Governor and a prominent figure in the Second World War coalition government headed by his old friend Winston Churchill.

But the lasting legacy of Nicolson and his wife Vita Sackville-West is the tale of their personal lives. Both bisexual, they pursued several same-sex affairs in their open marriage but somehow remained intensely in love with each other. Their shared love of Sissinghurst, and the outstanding garden they created there, has given us a gift enjoyed by millions.

We know about all this from several vivid books: Victoria Glendinning's classic biography *Vita*, the candid memoir *Portrait of a Marriage* by Harold and Vita's son Nigel, and *Sissinghurst*, the highly popular book and TV series by their grandson Adam Nicolson, who still lives there.

But this tale concerns the little-known haunting of Sissinghurst. There is no doubt about the special atmosphere of the ancient grounds. There is a *Secret Garden* sort of magic there. When I invited Harold's son Nigel Nicolson to give a talk at my Canterbury bookshop, he chose, unusually, to give just a commentary on a slide-show of the house and garden. I still remember seeing one slide in particular, of a girl clowning around with Nigel on the lawn on a hot summer's day. In the darkened bookshop café, the hairs on the back of my neck stood up as Nicolson's resonant old voice gently mused: 'Yes, and there's little Virginia Woolf messing around as usual ... she so loved our garden.'

Woolf's books are so evocative of time and the tricks it plays. Harold and Vita knew about these tricks too. In 1954, they told their friend Felix Seward, Chairman of the Ghost Club, that there was a ghost priest at Sissinghurst. Seward's successor at the Ghost Club, Peter Underwood, tracked down Nicolson to learn more, as he recounted in an obscure 1985 book, printed in Whitstable. He was invited for lunch at the great man's London club in the early 1960s. Sir Harold said he was 'utterly convinced' about the ghost priest, who had been walled up alive. Vita, he went on, sensed that the 'unquiet spirit' took comfort from the peace of the garden, which the couple had created out of wilderness. They had not seen the ghost, but many visitors had asked them about the sad 'reverend gentleman' whom they saw in the garden. Some others heard soft shuffling footsteps beside them as they walked the paths. To Mrs Hayter, Vita's trusted housekeeper, he was an accepted resident.

There is a final spooky end to this tale. Vita Sackville-West died in 1962, and Harold died in 1968. Psychic researcher Peter Underwood, described by the *Sunday Times* as 'the man who knows more about ghosts than anyone alive', stayed in touch with the staff at Sissinghurst. Nicolson had a habit of clicking his teeth with his tongue. The noise has been repeatedly heard in different parts of Sissinghurst by visitors who remember him, especially, Underwood says, young men.

STEEL WHEELS:
HOW THE ROLLING
STONES CAME TO BE

1960

In 1960, a young Adonis called Mick Jagger got on the train at Dartford, bound for London. An 18-year-old student at the London School of Economics, he carried four R&B records, including *The Best of Muddy Waters*. Such records were hard to come by but Jagger often sent cheques off to America for records, and he knew collectors such as Alexis Korner and the great Dave Godin, whose Bexleyheath house was an Aladdin's cave of rare vinyl. A languid youth of the same age called Keith Richards sat down in the same carriage. Although the two were both from Dartford and had known of each other, this was their first real meeting, because Richards, seeing Jagger's records, realised he had found a fellow enthusiast for the Blues. 'How did you get this stuff?' Richards first enquired. As the 1950s dark-blue slam-door diesel rumbled along, the two agreed to meet soon.'

 In retrospect, both men agreed that they never thought, 'Let's start a band', they just wanted to meet, listen to records and 'figure out how it was done'. If Dartford seems an unglamorous place for a legend to start, spare a thought for Penge boy Ronnie Wood and son of Neasden Charlie Watts. Poignantly, 40 years later, Jagger attended the opening of a new practice space and concert hall, a place with a mission to inspire an area which is still marred by poverty. Although opened, quaintly, by the Duke of Kent, it is called the Mick Jagger Centre.

HOW TO SOLVE A LOVE TRIANGLE

1961

In 1961 a man posing locally as Mr Barclay quietly got married at Folkestone's shabby registry office. The two witnesses, E. Pugsley and J. Bond, were either office staff or passers-by. I was agog when a customer in my Canterbury bookshop told me about this, the secret wedding of Nobel–prizewinner Samuel Beckett.

It is said that his *Waiting for Godot* is always being staged somewhere in the world. Critics still argue fiercely over the meaning of this strangely enjoyable work. Beckett preserved an intense privacy about both his work and his private life. So, what was he doing in Folkestone?

The master of 'absurdist' drama was trying to simplify the absurdity of his love life. Beckett had lived almost all his life in Paris, where James Joyce was his friend and mentor. In 1937 Joyce took him to dinner with the American art collector, Peggy Guggenheim. Beckett's offer to walk her home to her St Germain flat turned into a 12-day, champagne-fuelled session in bed. The relationship lasted a year but, like Olivier with Vivien Leigh, Beckett could not keep up with Peggy's sexual appetite. She was later to claim that she had bedded over 1,000 men and many women.

Peggy was in love with Sam, even saying she would give up her promiscuity to be his, but he wrote to a friend, 'There is a French girl also whom I am very fond of, and who is very good to me'. This was 37-year-old Suzanne Deschevaux-Dumesnil. Peggy wintrily said, 'She makes curtains. I make scenes,' a reference to her stormy disposition. Interviewed in 1973 Peggy reflected, 'I don't think he was in love with me for more than ten minutes. He couldn't make up his mind about anything. He wanted me around but did not want to have to do anything about it.' Suzanne was to be another victim of this existential diffidence.

The relationship with Suzanne, a strong-minded, teetotal, piano-playing socialist, was to last to the end of her life. Together they fought in the French resistance – the French government awarded Beckett a medal for his exploits, although typically he dismissed them as 'boy-scout stuff'. In later years she put up with his moaning and groaning, and his excessive boozing, and from 1956 onwards there was a long-term shadow, another woman, the Londoner Barbara Bray.

Bray was a young widow with two daughters. A BBC Radio drama editor, she was a brilliant and cultured linguist, confident enough to instruct Beckett on what he should read, and trusted by him as an editor. She received 700 letters from him. He destroyed all of hers, as he did any letters he received. She looked back, 'It took 30 seconds to fall in love with him … he had a voice like the ocean'. She was a mini-Peggy, remembered by a friend as 'unstoppable, effusive, almost manic'.

To Beckett's horror, in 1961 Bray, aged 36, decided to jack in her BBC job and live the bohemian life in Paris, near her love. Beckett had always compartmentalised his two women, seeing Bray on many London visits, but having Suzanne as his mainstay in Paris. Suzanne and Beckett were like an old married couple, holidaying together, travelling – even after Beckett became rich – on the Metro, and eating out in cheap restaurants. They both had austere tastes, and happily gave away a lot of money rather than be troubled by it. She often made her own clothes, and repaired his. He decided to secure his position with Suzanne, and quietly buttress himself against Bray's encroachment on his Paris life, by marrying the ageing Suzanne, now 61.

By now Beckett was big news, his legendary reclusiveness making his life all the more newsworthy. A fanfare would pain him and devastate Bray so he chose Folkestone for his nuptial venture. He drove his 2CV to Le Touquet, and then onto a Silver City Airways plane, which arrived at Lydd airport. The air ferry planes carried just three cars and some canvas seats – ideal for privacy. This short-lived Kent transport phenomenon collapsed when roll-on, roll-off car ferries started in the 1960s.

From Lydd he went to check in as Mr Barclay at Folkestone's Hotel Bristol, 3–4 The Leas, overlooking the sea. This now-demolished, 20-room hotel, built in the 1850s, was chosen for its obscurity, and here Beckett stayed for the fortnight that the law required to precede marriage in England. After the first night's dinner – Dover sole cooked to a mush and soggy vegetables – Sam dined at various local country pubs and loved them, especially the beer. He was mostly alone, as Suzanne only had to come over for the ceremony.

What a presence he must have made in those country pubs inland of Folkestone, ordering in his soft, oceanic Dublin brogue, then sitting alone with his striking, lined face and piercing green eyes. Harold Pinter recalled Sam's 'quick stride and insanely fast Citroen-driving'. Beckett worked on *Happy Days*, now a much-performed play, in the Hotel Bristol. Kentish names appealed to the poet in him: Borough Green and Sevenoaks entered *Happy Days*, and he used Ash and Snodland in other plays. There is no plaque on the bleak flats that have replaced the hotel. On a postcard home, he joked that his blood flowed more easily in the town of William Harvey – the discoverer of the human circulatory system.

Back in Paris, Beckett put his love triangle into a play, called *Play*, but his marriage had successfully defused

211

the three-way complexity; Barbara Bray got the message. She died in an Edinburgh nursing home in 2010, aged 85. Just before he died in 1989, a few months after his wife's death, Beckett confided to his biographer: 'I owe everything to Suzanne'.

INSECT JUNGLE

1964

Geoff Allen is one of Britain's foremost experts on bees, wasps and ants (aculeates). Rather than wondering, as many of us do, 'Does anything eat wasps?' he happily collects them, and their relatives, in all sizes. Allen got interested in aculeates as a Kentish lad, when the late great John Felton taught him to catch, mount and label them. Allen's masterpiece is the book *Bees, Wasps and Ants of Kent*. It draws on the work of many past entomologists, and on the private notebooks of Dr Gerald Dicker. Dicker, who does not feature on the internet, quietly studied Kent insects for decades. His notebooks were something of a Holy Grail for Kent entomology, and they were located especially for the book. Allen dedicated his book, touchingly, to his late wife Alison, 'who understood', he wrote, 'and patiently accepted my passion for these insects'. All the aculeate literature I have scanned points to one place in Kent: Dungeness, the largest area of shingle in Europe, with its clean air and miles of unspoiled habitat. And down there, Allen and his predecessors have uncovered exotic biodiversity.

A typical national rarity, which is quite common at Dungeness, is a *Myrmicine* ant which preys on its fellow insects. 'Small, dark and pugnacious', its jaws open wide enough to bite through human skin. As if this wasn't bad enough, during July, it takes flight. Even less principled is *Formica sanguinea*; large and aggressive, from its many-tunnelled fortress in a fallen tree trunk, it raids other ants' nests, bringing back the young to its trunk. Some it eats, the others it uses as slaves. As predatory but more subtle is *Solenopsis fugax*. It is so tiny – possibly Britain's smallest ant – that it builds nests, undetected, in nests of other ants. A true bounder, it steals the baby ants of its 'host', and feeds them to its own tiny young. Thought to be rare, it was first recorded in the 1850s, and last officially seen by old John Felton in 1964, but perhaps this evil micro-ant has just been overlooked because it is so small.

Kent wasps are as extraordinary. The spider wasp is thoroughly 'hyper', forever 'running about in an excited manner'; it is fast enough to catch many species of spider. A thrifty wasp, it takes its spider prey apart and hangs bits of them on low vegetation, as larders for future consumption. Kent's laziest wasp is the coastal rarity, recorded from Deal to Dungeness, *Evagetes pectinipes*. Keen on sex but uninterested in parenting, it is a cleptoparasite, that is, it lays eggs, cuckoo-like, in other species' nests. More constructive home-builders are Kent's mason wasps, which build with mud, and the carpenter wasp, which drills a cosy home in wood.

Kent bees generally have less warped collective minds than their ant and wasp cousins, but are as fascinating. The only really nasty Kent bee can be met at Dungeness. Intensely territorial, it spends much of its time patrolling for other species and quickly disabling them. It cannot be bothered to kill. It makes up a little for this chavvy streak by weaving its nest from hairs which it collects from the underside of the plant called lamb's ear. This ability to make a structure from raw plant hair gives it the name wool carder bee. The sheer painstaking dedication of Allen and the other insect recorders of the Kent Field Club is mind-boggling. The bee *Colletes halophilus* is a rarity of worldwide significance, but it is only distinguished by a) the lack of an apical fimbria on its gaster (central fringe on its abdomen) and b) that tell-tale 'sigmoidally [double-curved] outward curving second vein on the forewing'. And one can only marvel at how entomologists discovered the habits of Kent's mining bee. Small and black, it lives in ground burrows, which the female waterproofs with a mysterious secretion. As hair would get in the way of burrowing, it lacks the 'fur' on which other bees carry pollen. Instead, it carries pollen in its throat. And finally, for anyone who thinks Kent's insects are dull, there is the *Hylaeus* group of bees. Over 95 per cent of them are known to come from Kent: hairless and often yellow-faced, they have no great home-building talent, nor do they even aspire to parasitise other bees' homes. They are so weirdly powerless that one expert thinks that 'they may be a reversal in evolution'.

THE VANISHING
HITCHHIKER
1968 ONWARDS

Despite our rational façade, we all trade in myths. Does fast food contain cat meat? Do alligators live in New York's sewers? In our millions, we shiver at stories about aliens, vampires, zombies and doppelgängers. As the work of Carl Jung explains, these myths help us to defuse our deepest fears by bringing them into the open. Myths have a psychic use, beyond mere sensationalism, so they endure, mutating for each generation. Even in pre-digital times, they sprouted simultaneously in different cultures, providing evidence of a collective mind. Alien abduction stories have been especially universal. Well-authenticated non-mythological evidence for this mass animal consciousness comes from British blue tits in the 1960s. They all learned, within a few weeks, how to pierce the foil tops of doorstop milk bottles, to get at the cream.

The classic study of modern legends is Professor Jan Brunvand's *The Vanishing Hitchhiker: Urban Legends and Their Meanings*. Blue Bell Hill near Maidstone, the A229, has Britain's most persistent hitchhiker mythos. It is an otherworldly place. Being on the crest of the Downs, it has a micro-climate, its busy road often afflicted with hair-raising pockets of sudden thick fog or snow. You must see its spookiness to believe it – and those who have will understand.

In 1974, Maurice Goodenough came into Rochester police station to report that he had driven into a girl who had rushed out in front of him on the hill. No body was found, but the hitchhiker's habit was established: in 1992, Ian Sharpe 'hit' the girl, who looked calmly at him before disappearing under the car. Chris Dawkins reported a similar horror in the same year. He went to Maidstone police station, where the police were used to such reports. A 1994 TV documentary analysed some of the scores of accounts of this 'vanishing' girl. No body has ever been found.

THE UNIVERSITY THAT COLLAPSED

1974

The creation of the University of Kent at Canterbury was a great act of 1960s hopefulness. The new campus, on a hill north of Canterbury, was a bold 1964 design in concrete and breeze block, in a style called brutalism. The original architect, Lord Holford, was a typical 'concrete crusader', famous as the creator of the new village of Berinsfield back in 1960. The usually reserved architectural historian Sir Nikolaus Pevsner, despite being a devoted modernist, was disgusted by Berinsfield. 'A huge council estate,' he spluttered, 'of the most dismal kind, sprawling out aimlessly across dreary streets.' But brutalism and concrete were firmly in vogue and so in 1961 Holford, a Boer, was given one of Britain's most sensitive sites: Paternoster Square, right next to St Paul's Cathedral. Holford delivered a disastrous concrete jungle, which appalled tourists and depressed Londoners. One Mayor of London called it 'a ghastly monolithic construction without character'. By 1980, it was hard to fill leases in the windswept Paternoster Square, and by 2003 the whole square, Holford's masterpiece, had been completely redeveloped.

Holford's University of Kent design was described by one fawning lecturer as 'a series of grandiloquent words in bold capitals'. Less charitably, the authoritative *Buildings of England* series called the complex 'uncommunicative ... bitty ... an ivory tower ... with exposed concrete beams'.

Holford's design, then, was not an aesthetic success. In addition, a serious technical flaw was to come to light. The disued Canterbury to Whitstable Railway tunnel ran under the University. The official University history pompously claimed that the architects 'were of course well aware of the problems posed by the tunnel, and at a very early stage the advice of civil engineering consultants was sought'. Despite this, in 1974, the main Cornwallis Building collapsed, taking with it the footbridge linking it to the Gulbenkian Theatre. Holford's concrete was too much for the hand-dug 1830 railway tunnel, which had caved in. The architects claimed that they had regularly inspected the tunnel, and so it was that the University history, in a splendidly unscientific piece of whitewash, explained the collapse as 'the application of the renowned Murphy's Law'.

Quite apart from this costly cock-up by the arrogant Holford, the University, supposedly a cultural institution, then irrevocably damaged the world's first passenger railway tunnel: rather than repairing it, they pumped concrete into several sections. The whole Canterbury to Whitstable line is of world heritage significance. The tunnel was designed by George Stephenson, Thomas Telford engineered the new Whitstable Harbour, and Robert Stephenson's legendary locomotive, the *Invicta* – now in Canterbury Museum – was built for the line. Isambard Kingdom Brunel was an early, admiring visitor. Holford had a peerage, and many academic honours, but his shoddy project management and Stalinist design sense contrast sadly with the standards of these great Victorian engineers.

THE MEDICAL MARVEL IN A KENT DITCH

1978

Leeches have been used since ancient times for blood-letting. It was thought that they sucked out bad blood and left the good. The practice became so established that British leeches became increasingly rare. By 1802, Wordsworth could use the leech-gatherer's words as a symbol of wistfulness: 'they have dwindled long ... yet still I persevere and find them where I may'. By 1833, 42 million leeches a year had to be imported into Britain. Eerily tough, they can live in Antarctica or Borneo, get (literally) right up your nose and into unspeakable places, or puncture a rhino's hide. Historically, they were difficult to administer safely. After their 'meal', bleeding would not stop, owing to chemicals in the leech's saliva. Although the traditional way to remove them was by a lighted cigarette applied to their body, this had a drawback: the shock made them vomit their meal, and previous meals, into the wound. Of course, in the modern sterile hospital there is no place for these nasty bloodsuckers, with their 100 saw-like teeth on three Y-shaped jaws: or is there?

Our tale moves to 1978, and a very hot, clear day near Dungeness. Local man William Bartram was out walking his dog when panting Fido took a leap into one of the area's many water-filled ditches. A vigorous shake later, and the walk continued, but something remained on the dog, firmly attached and swelling in size as it sucked blood: the until recently 'extinct' British leech. Scientists were incredulous. The leech must be an accidental escape. But searches discovered over 10,000 leeches at this site.

Then something even stranger happened. Surgeons around the world were becoming increasingly skilled at reattaching lost body parts, but their attempts were often in vain (or perhaps that should be 'in vein'!) because blood circulation failed to re-establish itself. Leeches were indeed to re-enter the modern hospital. They are now frequently used, as their saliva contains both anaesthetic and anti-coagulant. In Australia, a young surfer awoke in hospital after a shark attack to see that his hand had been amputated. But a determined Vietnamese doctor thought of leeches; the hand was successfully reattached and came to life with the help of the little bloodsuckers. 'After the initial freak-out,' the surfer said, he ended up 'applying the little critters myself'. In Boston, USA, the success of an operation to reattach a five-year-old's ear after a dog attack was dependent on leeches. The leeches always seemed to leave clean incisions, confirming the findings of a twelfth-century Baghdad physician, who used them to clean up after operations.

Back in Dungeness, something even stranger happened in 1998. Pharmaceuticals giant Glaxo Wellcome funded a two-year leech hunt. These modern leech-gatherers used the same technique as Wordsworth's gatherer, standing in the water and stamping their feet for 20 minutes until leeches, aware of a warm mammal, swam towards their legs. By 2000, Glaxo had found 85 leech locations on Dungeness and Romney Marsh: the biggest colony in Europe, now protected by legislation.

There is one more, even stranger, part of this tale. In 2008, Hollywood actress Demi Moore admitted one of her beauty secrets: she goes to Austria, has a bath in turps and is then serially leeched. 'You feel it bite,' she said, 'and you go, "You little bastard!" but then you work on your breathing and relax. Afterwards you feel years younger.'

The humble leech has come a long way, from parasite to surgical aid and superstar accessory. And it may have other uses. In the 1960s, my father started a long correspondence in *The Times* about some of these (much to the disgust of scientists), especially their ability to be barometers, predicting storms by rising up a bell jar – a phenomenon which has now been scientifically validated. It is lucky for us that their biggest colony clung on in a quiet Kent backwater through all the years of 'extinction'.

KATE BUSH
AND KENTISH MAGIC

1985

'I was unhappy at school, I couldn't wait to leave, I became introverted, my friends sometimes ignored me completely, and that would upset me badly.' Even the music teacher at St Joseph's convent school, now Bexley College, saw little in Kate Bush. In the panto, she was cast as a shepherdess: the singing roles were given to others. But Bush was quietly writing songs and playing music at home, at East Wickham Farm near Bexleyheath. There she learned piano at 11 and, remarkably, wrote several songs which later became famous. At 13, she drafted 'The Man with the Child in His Eyes'. She made demo tapes, one of which found its way to Pink Floyd's Dave Gilmour. He was so impressed that he visited the farmhouse in 1973 to make a more professional tape of her music. Then, when she was 16, he paid for her to record in EMI's legendary Air studios in Oxford Street. In the same year, EMI signed her and, incidentally, she became a vegetarian, quietly telling her GP dad, 'I won't eat life.'

It was her artistic, eccentric family setting which nurtured her talent. Her school knew little of it. Indeed, as her biographer Graeme Thompson says, while all this was going on, she was still quietly going to school in her regulation red knickers, reluctantly attending violin lessons but not telling anyone about her pop-folk talent. For Bush and her talented two brothers, a large barn behind East Wickham Farm provided a peaceful space for playing, dressing up, dancing and singing. The Kent countryside bred her: both the safety of the old farm and the trips all over Kent in search of gigs, dances and folk music.

Her rise was stellar and fast. In 1978, at 19, she was the most photographed woman in Britain. In that year, a schoolfriend, hearing of her music on the radio, expected a classical piece, not the mould-breaking 'Wuthering Heights'. In her typically private way, Bush rejected the bits of fame she disliked: EMI made her do a tour: she never did one again all her life. They photographed her as a sex symbol: she became a cheesecloth-and-jeans-clad semi-recluse. They put her into a film: she called it 'a load of bollocks'. After some years in and out of windowless London studios, clockwatching, she felt exhausted and burned out. She was in such an artistic trough that *NME* featured her in a 'Where are they now?' feature. Her complex, much-synthesised album *The Dreaming* got mixed reviews. A Caribbean holiday did little to revitalise her. Realising that West Kent rural backwaters had bred her talent, she went back there, buying a cottage near Sevenoaks and doing a lot of gardening. Then she installed recording facilities in her childhood home, East Wickham Farm. Just like the old days, her poet brother would drop in with a mug of tea and listen to sessions, and her dad would send out for curries to keep the flow going, often late into the night. Her Kentish boyfriend Del was the sound engineer.

The resultant 1985 album, *Hounds of Love*, adorned with atmospheric pictures of Bush taken by her brother, remains a phenomenon. Quickly knocking Madonna's *Like A Virgin* off the Number 1 spot, it went on to sell 3 million copies. In 2002, it was voted the third greatest album ever by a female artist and in 2010 it was remastered to renewed acclaim.

Like *The Dreaming*, *Hounds of Love* was also highly experimental, but, rather than being fuelled by an urban EMI set-up, it came from a rural peacefulness. Once again, Bush could lie upstairs in the barn and look out of the old round window at moonlit countryside.

THE MOST HAUNTED VILLAGE IN ENGLAND?

1989

Pluckley, near Ashford, acquired this accolade back in the mists of time, and in 1989 it entered *The Guinness Book of Records*. The title remains unchallenged, as modern ghost hunters have been delighted by Pluckley's veritable smorgasbord of the paranormal.

Several TV programmes have featured overnight stays in the Screaming Woods, where a ghost's bloodcurdling screams rend the air. One of the most frequently reported spectres is of highwayman Robert du Bois, who is seen, as he was killed, skewered to a tree at Fright Corner. The Black Horse pub can only boast a poltergeist, but that does not stop it hosting its 'Frightday Night' spooky suppers, with inevitable offers on 'spirits'.

In the Old Bakery in 1976, owner Mike Henderson unwittingly unleashed some unpleasantness when he moved a Victorian fireplace, exposing an older hearth. Icy 'chill spots' started to affect the room. Visitors frequently heard someone upstairs walking from the door to the fireplace, when Mike knew there was no one up there.

But most of the manifestations centre on the Dering family, owners of the manor, which burned down in 1950. A past Lord Dering was so distressed at the death of his beautiful young wife that, in a sad attempt to preserve her, he buried her in the family vault in an oak coffin, inside three lead coffins, with a red rose on her breast. The site of the Dering Manor is haunted by the 'White Lady', who holds a red rose. Uncomfortably, hammering sounds have issued from the vault. The 2010 *Penguin Book of Ghosts* records that in the 1970s psychic researchers spent a night in the vault. Next day, they told the vicar how boring it had been: 'We were quite glad your dog came to join us from time to time.' 'Actually,' the vicar replied, 'I don't have a dog.'

In the churchyard, the 'Red Lady' is another Lady Dering. She searches eternally for the grave of her baby who, having died at birth unbaptised, was refused a place in the family vault. A Tudor monk who pined away for love of Lord Dering's mistress has been seen in the garden of a house called Greystones, most recently by a boy on holiday who was just about to photograph the house.

There seems to be almost too many ghosts in Pluckley, an embarrassment of psychic riches, a tsunami of spooks. But, in defence of these tales, many go back a long way, and have some startling circumstantial detail. Like the old Victorian gypsy woman, a watercress-seller, who fell asleep in a haystack with her lit claypipe. She burned to death, but was repeatedly seen at the spot. More recently, a red glow has been reported there.

In 1973, Ghost Club President, Peter Underwood, was told about the unusual bedroom ghost in a house called Church Gates. It walked through the wall and into the upstairs room next door. The two houses used to be one, the wall being a late addition. He also met Aileen Beckworth, who was plagued by knockings from her fireplace for years. She 'nearly dropped her tea tray' one day when a grey figure glided past her into her kitchen.

Readers with access to the Internet can trawl the rest: the screams of the man who fell down a claypit, the phantom soldier and the miller who won't leave his mill. Someone has even reported the obligatory empty coach and horses clattering through the village.

Is there any truth in Hamlet's warning? 'There are more

things in heaven and earth, Horatio, than are dreamed of in your philosophy.' If there is – and how is it that we all know someone who has seen a ghost? – then Pluckley, even stripped of its less credible tales, may well be the Piccadilly Circus of haunted England.

ALAN CLARK IN THE BOOT

1992

Alan Clark was probably the richest MP of his day, the lord of medieval Saltwood Castle near Hythe, as well as owning tracts of Scotland and an alpine chalet. This wealth, coupled with an extraordinary intellect, meant that he usually did and said pretty much what he wanted. He died in Canterbury in 1999 but fortunately his witty and refreshing diaries live on.

The indiscretions are legendary. He called Africa 'bongo-bongo land' and Michael Heseltine 'the sort of chap who buys his own furniture'. Made a minister by Margaret Thatcher, he designed the most effective defence cuts of the century, but addressed the Commons while drunk. He once rejected a lunchtime meeting, writing on departmental notepaper that 'this will be impossible as at lunchtime I am usually involved in Ugandan discussions' (*Private Eye* code for improper activity with a woman).

Much of this rakish behaviour, celebrated in the John Hurt/Jenny Agutter biopic, stemmed from fear of boredom and age, and of the march of what he called 'the greys'. Behind it all, Clark was a sensitive soul, whose book *The Donkeys*, about murderously incompetent Great War generals, remains an anti-war classic, inspiring the 1960s musical *Oh What a Lovely War!* And he was fiercely protective of the natural world. This lesser-known 'green' Clark was the man loved by Jane, the wife whom he had met and become romantically obsessed with on Folkestone beach when she was just 14. I had long conversations with them both, after Clark gave two author talks in my Canterbury bookshop, with what he called its 'low-ceilinged, fetid rooms' and 'bolshy audience'. We talked wide-rangingly, from history – he suggested that I stay at Saltwood Castle and write its history – to nature. When I enthused about Kent's nightingales and gave them Richard Mabey's book on the birds, they excitedly hatched a plan to turn part of the castle grounds into 'nightingale country'. Talking together like this, they were loving, idealistic and visionary. They nurtured a series of injured birds in the kitchen at Saltwood. Recently, both had joined crowds of dreadlocked protesters at Dover docks, demonstrating against live veal calf exports. Even now, the animal liberationist purple ribbons flutter on bushes at the Dover roundabout.

Like many, Margaret Thatcher expected Clark to be a traditional Tory. 'You fox-hunt, don't you?' asked the Prime Minister once of her new minister. When Clark explained that he was a vegetarian who banned the hunt from crossing his lands, she questioned such a stance, pointing out that he must be wearing leather shoes? No, he avoided those too.

Clark's philandering was indefensible but Jane wrote, as he lay dying in the Kent and Canterbury Hospital, of 'my soul mate of 41 years, my lover, my friend, my companion'. Just before he died, when he could hear her but only squeeze her hand, she spoke of what she would do in the castle grounds, of 'the woodland walk and the brambles on the cistus bank'. 'We were always such a good team,' she wrote soon afterwards. He had a 'green' burial at Saltwood, in a shroud rather than a coffin.

So the 'raving Tory' Clark persona is a simplification. But so too is the 'Jane Clark the doormat' theory: she was spectacular when pushed too far. On one such occasion, she grabbed a ceremonial sword from a display on the castle wall and hurled it straight at him. Another revolt occurred when his affair with 'the coven' was exposed. He had slept with a judge's wife and two of her daughters. In public, Jane lamented the way the coven sold their story to tabloids, observing, 'What do you expect when you sleep with below-stairs types?' To avoid the press pack waiting outside Saltwood Castle gates, Clark hid in the car boot as Jane drove home. Jane, who was by now publicly referring to her husband as 'the S, H, one, T', parked in the courtyard and left him for the evening in the boot as she went inside her home.

The Clarks loved each other and their Kentish patch with a depth which makes this one of Kent's most beautifully strange tales.

THE ROADWORKS THAT CHANGED HISTORY

1992

I like Dover. It is a transit point, a place of flux, of holidays and of crime, joy and grief.

I am in a minority in my affection. The town is, according to the *Rough Guide*, 'unprepossessing'. *Lonely Planet* is harsher, describing 'a run-down air of decay'. Bill Bryson dealt it a killer blow with an achingly funny account of his stay in a dreadful B&B there, run by the unforgiving 'Mrs Smegma'.

Noisy road-widening excavations completed the bleak scene. Here, in late September 1992, archaeologist Keith Parfitt was near the end of his dig. The Roman harbour wall had been discovered and recorded, enough of a milestone in any digger's career. But as he knocked off for lunch a colleague shouted out that he had spotted some man-made woodwork at an impossibly deep level, way below the Roman wall. Parfitt soon realised it was part of a boat and one which, at this depth, must be incredibly ancient. It was indeed the world's oldest maritime craft, preserved so well by bacteria-repelling silt that, in time, the marks of six different sorts of tools would be found on the wood.

The road-making workers were about to return from lunch, so Parfitt made a series of panicked phone calls to ever-higher authorities to get them stopped. Reluctantly, the Department of Transport, represented no doubt by an official resembling Mr Grimsdale in a Norman Wisdom film, agreed to halt the roadworks for just six days. Dover Harbour Board offered a crane to lift the boat. Crowds of locals gathered. Experts from the British Museum and National Maritime Museum arrived, just like the FBI in the movies. They confirmed that this was a find of worldwide significance. Sadly, about a third of the 40ft (12.2m) boat had to be left under Townwall Street, unexcavated; but in pouring October rain the harbour crane raised the craft and it was put in a tank nearby.

How could it be preserved? In 1937, in Yorkshire, a similar boat had been found but, exposed to air, it decayed rapidly. After consulting the Mary Rose Trust, who had preserved a Tudor warship, the Dover boat was soaked in wax for two years, and then freeze-dried at minus-25 degrees Celsius.

The tale gets even stranger. Radiocarbon analysis put the boat at 3,500 years old. When it was on the water, Stonehenge was in ritual use and the Egyptian Pharaoh Rameses the Great (Ozymandias in Shelley's poem) was in power. The boat was found beached quite far up Dover's River Dour, and it had a river-punt shape. No nails or dowels were used: rope made of twisted yew branches held the planks together. It seemed a flimsy vessel. This evidence, combined with a fairly dim academic view of ancient seafaring abilities, seemed to make it an inland river craft. But two discoveries under the microscope changed all that. A lump of shale in the boat was found to be from Dorset, and the hull bore traces of sea-dwelling molluscs.

Despite previous assumptions, this boat was seagoing, having travelled to Dorset, France and perhaps further afield. The boat confirmed, the £80 official report was to say, 'the existence of routine traffic between Britain and Europe in Bronze Age times': it is the first known cross-channel ferry and it seated 18 paddlers.

The find's location gives this tale a further riveting twist. It would have been difficult to get the boat as far up the shallow River Dour as the spot where it was found, and furthermore that spot would have been a useless place to have it. Close inspection of the boat's vicinity revealed butchered animal bones, scorched stones, and all the debris of a great ritual feast, held in the boat. Also, oddly, the craft was beached and partly dismantled while still perfectly usable. Like the Sutton Hoo ship in Suffolk 2,000 years later, the boat was probably beached for a wake when a great leader died, at a spiritually significant spot or, simply, near his home. Academics always think of trade or war but maybe Dorset was the best family holiday the tribal leader ever had?

Buried in the dense thickets of the official report, one of the 39 authors is someone who knows all about rates of organic decomposition. He must be at the top of many dinner party lists. He discovered that the boat was carefully lifted to its position on the river bank, next to a village (examining insect remains, even the exact flora of the area is known). The boat, he goes on, would have been covered up by silt, not over decades, *but in just a few years.* 'What!?' I spluttered into my coffee upon reading this. Surely the family of the deceased would not have unintentionally dumped this elegant, still-useful boat, replete with memories, by a village in cattle fields, and, having had a feast in it, just left it there to watch it disappear into silt a bit more each day? Surely these ancient Kentish navigators meant us to find the boat intact. They deliberately positioned it so that it would quickly be preserved for millennia. Their Egyptian contemporaries were similarly determined to preserve memories of their leaders for us to see. In Cairo Museum, we can still look upon the mummified face of Ozymandias (Rameses), and he only looks slightly worse than I do on a Monday morning.

This puts a new light on that September scene in Dover, as experts ran around and the street was cordoned off. Rather than academics stumbling on an abandoned ship, we were doing what those old navigators intended, viewing sacred memories of our significant ancestor. If you believe

235

in these things, you can imagine the spirits of the Bronze Age family standing outside Jays nightclub (these ancients would have understood its Dionysian purpose well). They are watching us with satisfaction across all the fuss of the last 3,000 years of art and warfare, as we come to appreciate their craftsmanship, their seamanship and their love of one of their chieftains.

Archaeologists seem to be continually discovering that our ancient ancestors were far more sophisticated than the 'ugga-ugga' cavemen featured in many a comedy sketch. These Kent roadworks led to a discovery which has changed our view of our ancient selves. A little Australian girl ends this tale. She recently wrote in the Dover Boat Gallery visitors' book: 'It proves we were smart.'

THE TEABAG
FUNDAMENTALIST
GHOST

2006

Martins is an old East Kent chain of clothes stores, which
finally closed its last branch in 2002. It was run along
the lines of the sitcom *Are You Being Served?* which was
itself based on the now-defunct Simpsons in Piccadilly.
The Canterbury branch features in the classic Powell and
Pressburger film *A Canterbury Tale*. Situated in a listed
four-floor building in St Margaret's Street, the building
is a veritable palimpsest of history. The basement houses
a Roman bath-house floor, the ground floor medieval
masonry, the first floor hidden Tudor timberwork and the
shopfront is Regency-style.

If ever there was a happy haunting-ground for spirits,
it would be here. Sure enough, the building, which
became a Waterstone's bookshop in 1990 with me as the
manager, is awash with psycho-kinetic activity. The cash-
office manager, a severely practical and prim middle-aged
lady with no interest in phenomena, was once locked
in the building alone all night. When I rescued her, she
was a gibbering wreck. She fled the building and the job
immediately: we kept her attaché case and coat for years,
but she never returned to collect them. Eventually, I prised
her locked case open with a screwdriver, in case I could
contact her via her mobile phone list. All I found was a BLT
on rye in an advanced state of decomposition. Philip Carr-
Gomm, respected author of the *Book of English Magic*

(2009) and the man chosen by the government to write the pagan strand of the national curriculum, identified a naiad, or water spirit, in the now underground spring which fed the Roman baths. The spring creates a permanent damp patch on a basement wall. The Romans often took over sites of archaic worship. In a separate basement incident, bookseller Gavin Pilgrim was handed a book he was searching for by an invisible incarnation. But the top-floor coffee shop is the real epicentre for discarnate entities, the paranormal hub.

Just as Welsh psychic Stephen O'Brien began his author talk in the café, all electrics blew, including lights, escalator, a mains-fed calculator and the air-conditioning. The aircon engineer next day showed me melted copper piping and said, 'Look at this: someone's been up 'ere with a soldering iron, mate.' His bill was £11,300. O'Brien's account is in his *Visions of Another World.*

The café had opened in Martins in 1987, and Waterstone's kept it open, as, with its rooftop view and home-made scones, it had a large Kentish and international following. The regulars naturally became quite proprietorial about the menu. When Waterstone's asked swish London tea experts Whittard to run the café, they spent £25,000 refitting it and declared it a teabag-free zone, offering scores of loose-tea types, even monkey-picked oolong, the leaf which grows so inaccessibly that trained apes pick it. One old regular was particularly unhappy about the loose tea. After her sad death, teapots regularly shattered. Always the same table. The carpet got so stained with tea that Whittards repeatedly replaced the carpet tiles around that table. They complained to the crockery supplier, who nobly replaced the whole pot 'fleet', to no avail. I was present at several of the disturbances, which became so frequent as to escape remark. One smart female guest had to be offered reimbursement for her tea-splashed clothes. One day the ghost 'went tactical'. A pile of plates smashed onto the floor one by one as waitresses watched in disbelief. They later denied a ghost, preferring, like many when confronted with such bold manifestations, not to be spooked. But I was there, I checked the shelf, which was completely firm, and I heard the plates drop rhythmically, smashing one by one, and saw the astonished staff.

In 2009, Whitstable-based Chives took over the café, using tea bags.

Not a single teapot has hit the floor since.

KENT'S EXTRAORDINARY DRAGONFLIES

2010

The marriage of John and Gill Brook is a great blessing to the dragonflies of Kent. Gill not only shares John's expertise, she beautifully illustrates these insects. Together, they produced *The Dragonflies of Kent*. This work benefits from the Brooks' particular talent: the identification of dragonflies from the cast-off skin, or exuviae, of their aquatic larvae. Although the Brooks allege that this is an easy and enjoyable pursuit, when one sees their illustrations of these shrivelled husks among the reeds, one can only marvel at their persistence.

Dragonflies are wholly beneficial. Although they only live for a few weeks, they have been zipping around at about 49ft (15m) per second for millions of years: they saw dinosaurs. They are beautiful, they don't sting and they eat mosquitoes and midges. Superstitious bumpkins call them 'adder's servants' or 'the devil's darning needle', but Kent is blessed with a weird profusion of these wrongly maligned aerial acrobats. Why? The Brooks tell us: the climate is warm, wetlands are frequent and Europe is nearby.

The story of the Small Red-Eyed Damselfly is a heart-warming one. A known European immigrant, in 2001 the Brooks found its exuviae – evidence of egg-laying – at, of all places indeed, Bluewater Shopping Centre. Dragonflies, it seems, are no nature-reserve snobs!

Long may they continue to survive, and thrive, in Kent.

£110,000
TO RESTORE A FROCK
2011

In old age, the actress Ellen Terry wrote, 'The past is now to me like a story in a book.' No wonder, for Ellen's life was, as her biographer Michael Holroyd concluded, 'like a fairy story'. It's hard to recapture just what a sensation she was, the undisputed queen of theatre, and a woman of animal magnetism. To a fellow actress, she had 'the proportions of a goddess and the airy lightness of a child'. Oscar Wilde, who wrote a poem about her hair and lips, saw her in a carriage 'one dreary, wet London night'. Thereafter, that street was enchanted for him. Even a vicar, a London neighbour, noted how the whole street came alive as she left her house, lapsing into everyday-ness once she had gone. Bram Stoker, the author of *Dracula*, thought her the embodiment of beauty; to H.G. Wells she was a goddess; Thomas Hardy tried and failed to put her otherness into words; and Virginia Woolf simply wanted her to be Queen. Ellen, the great Shakespearean actress, had come a long way from her humble show-business childhood; on her birth certificate her father's occupation was simply 'comedian'.

This beauty got her into a marriage, at just 16, to G.F. Watts, the painter, who was 46. At this time, Watts' picture of her, *Choosing*, was painted. It is one of Britain's most-loved and most erotically charged paintings. The pioneer photographer Julia Cameron also immortalised Ellen at

16, with her portrait 'Sadness'. Unhappy in her marriage, she soon escaped, moving in with an architect for the next six years without, scandalously, getting divorced from Watts. In all, she was eventually married three times and had numerous lovers. Ellen lived all aspects of her life with passion, and, naturally, she occasionally came unstuck. For instance, she took over a large London theatre to stage modern drama such as Ibsen and Shaw, but the venture flopped. However, the same romantic determination gained her the happiest home she ever had, a place where she found peace for 28 years, up to her death in 1928. Ellen saw Smallhythe Place, near Tenterden, when it was a dilapidated shepherd's cottage. She asked the shepherd, who had no intention of moving, to get in touch should he ever change his mind. Some time later, Ellen received an unsigned postcard with three words on it: 'House for Sale'; she purchased it immediately. (Her children shared her passionate intensity; a daughter lived on at Smallhythe in a pioneer gay ménage, usually dressed in corduroy trousers and tam-o'-shanter hat, while her son Gordon, a stage designer, fathered 13 children by eight women.) Happily for us, Smallhythe is now open to the public.

In 1888, Ellen Terry acted Lady Macbeth, with long-time acting partner and Platonic love Henry Irving. The production was just one of the artistic fireworks which lit up that *fin de siècle*. Oscar Wilde's magical *Happy Prince* was just out, so was the unexpurgated Burton translation of the *Arabian Nights*, and the first story about a cocaine-addicted detective called Sherlock Holmes. To portray Lady Macbeth's seductive evil, Ellen wore a green, iridescent dress made from thousands of wings from the jewel beetle – these wings are naturally shed throughout the beetle's life. She loved the dress, purring to a girlfriend in the dressing room: 'It's so easy on me … I don't even need a corset.' By 2006, the dress – on display at Smallhythe – was in a sorry state. It had crossed the Atlantic several times with

Ellen, and she was notorious for being late and dressing frantically. The National Trust spent £110,000 restoring it, and it went back on display in 2011. The irresistibly named Zenzie Tinker was in charge, and she used green-dyed tissue, made in Japan, to support the remaining beetle wings, stuck with glue. Finding extra beetle wings was a challenge, but an antique dealer in Tenterden donated a box of them.

Recent discoveries about the jewel beetle shed more light on this tale. It is attracted to forest fires. Sensing them even 50 miles (80.5km) away, it hurries towards them, so that it can lay eggs in the predator-free environment of a post-inferno zone. This unconventional beetle was a natural partner for the fearless Ellen Terry.

THE LAST DAYS OF A SECRETIVE CRAFT

2015

In November 2015 I tracked down the last practitioner of a secretive Kentish craft, a speciality unique to the Tunbridge Wells area. Peter Benjamin lives in Tonbridge but has no Internet presence, no mobile phone, and no answerphone. As he explained to me, he has enough work to last a lifetime so he has no need to advertise. Even thus far under the radar – darker than the darknet – he lamented that television reporters had twice got to him. I got his number by winning the trust of an aged Kentish antiques dealer, explaining that I wanted to tell the public the tale of a craft Kent should be proud of – the making of Tunbridge ware, a form of carpentry using tiny pieces of wood. Intricate patterns and scenes are depicted by using different-coloured wood from up to 120 tree species. Gluing them together is an art in itself, quite apart from carving and finding the wood.

The origins are lost in the mists of time, but it all started in the ancient damp forests of the Weald. When one of Queen Elizabeth's courtiers, Lord North, asked a local for a drink from a stream, he was handed a finely carved bowl. By 1697 a visitor to Tunbridge Wells noticed 'shops full of the curious wooden ware this place is noted for'. Trashy German 'strapware' and Italian 'Sorrento-ware' mimicked Tunbridge ware but with cheap veneer, and even – *quelle horreur* – dyed wood. True Tunbridge ware achieved colours naturally. A deep green came from 'green oak' – fallen logs discoloured by a rare Wealden fungus.

When Tunbridge Wells became a popular spa town, Tunbridge ware boxes became the town's characteristic souvenir: Jane Austen kept several on her dressing table, and mentioned them in her novel *Emma*. By 1840 just a few Tunbridge Wells families ran the industry, competing fiercely. The clans even discouraged marrying 'outsiders', as a way of keeping their trade secrets. They would not even pool their skills to make a table for Queen Victoria: they drew lots. The winning Barton family ostentatiously sourced a rare Brazilian tree, of tool-busting hardness. But the Burrows family fought back, inventing a mosaic method, which gave a 3-D effect. A disaffected Burrows apprentice defected to the Nye family and blew the secret technique. The Nyes were chosen to represent Tunbridge ware at the 1851 Great Exhibition.

Time heals all feuds, and by 1939 all the firms had merged into one, unfashionably opposing the age of mass-production. When a bomb hit the last workshop the owner was 'too discouraged' to carry on. The art lingered on as a cottage industry.

In the mid-twentieth century, Peter Benjamin visited Henry Littleton, one of the last survivors of the ware-making families. On the doorstep of his house in Rye, Littleton scorned Benjamin's claim to be making Tunbridge ware and tested him by asking what his glue was made of. Getting the wrong answer, Littleton slammed the door shut. Weeks later, he called Benjamin, apologised and invited him back. He was terminally ill, and agreed to pass on his secrets, even handing over a large piece of green oak. Benjamin treasures this piece, and has now trained his dog to sniff out the fungally-tinted wood on wet walks near Tonbridge. A new Tunbridge ware box can take two years to make and sell for up to £4,000. Hopefully the craft will be revived in the future, but Benjamin is now an old man, and has no apprentice.

BIBLIOGRAPHY

Abell, Henry, *History of Kent* (Kentish Express, Ashford,1898)

Allen, G.W., *Bees, Wasps and Ants of Kent* (Kent Field Club,Maidstone, 2009)

Anon, *Arden of Faversham* (New Mermaids, 2007)

Ashbee, Paul, *Kent in Prehistoric Times* (Tempus, Stroud, 2005)

Barham-Kingston Women's Institute, *The History of Barham* (Cobnut Press, Barham, 2005)

Bennett, Paul, Clark, Peter, Hicks, Alison and Rady, Jonathan, *At the Great Crossroads: Prehistoric, Roman and Medieval Discoveries on the Isle Of Thanet* (English Heritage, London, 2008)

Bowden, Hugh, *Mystery Cults in the Ancient World* (Thames and Hudson, London, 2010)

Brentnall, Margaret, *The Cinque Ports and Romney Marsh* (John Gifford, London, 1972)

Brookes, Stuart, Harrington, Sue, *The Kingdom and People of Kent, AD 400–1066* (History Press, Stroud, 2010)

Brunvand, Jan, *The Vanishing Hitchhiker* (WW Norton, New York, 1981)

Byrne, Paula, *Mad World, Evelyn Waugh and the Secrets of Brideshead* (Harper Collins, London, 2009)

Church, Richard, *Kent's Contribution* (Adams and Dart, Bath, 1972)

Clancy, John, *The Story of Sheppey* (History Press, Stroud, 2009)

Clark, Peter (Ed), *The Dover Bronze Age Boat* (English Heritage, London, 2004)

Clements, Jonathan (compiler), *Darwin's Notebook* (History Press, Stroud, 2009)

Foley, Michael, *Front-Line Kent* (History Press, Stroud, 2010)

Gardiner, Dorothy, *Companion into Kent* (Methuen, London, 1934)

Gillies, Midge, *Amy Johnson, Queen of the Air* (Orion, London 2003)

Glendinning, Victoria, *Vita* (Weidenfeld and Nicolson, London, 1983)

Gribbin, John, *Darwin* (Simon and Schuster, London, 1995)

Hague, William, *William Pitt* (Harper Collins, London, 2004)

Hasted, Edward, *The History and Topographical Survey of the County of Kent* (Canterbury, 1779)

Hill, Rosemary, *God's Architect: Pugin* (Allen Lane, London, 2007)

Hillier, Caroline, *The Bulwark Shore* (Methuen, London, 1980)

Holroyd, Michael, *A Strange Eventful History: The Dramatic Lives of Ellen Terry, Henry Irving and their families* (Chatto, London, 2008)

Hughes, David, *Flying Past: A History of Sheppey Aviation* (History Press, Stroud, 2009)

Jansen, Leo, Luijten, Hans and Baker, Nienke, *Vincent Van Gogh – The Letters: The Complete Illustrated and Annotated Edition* (5 vols, Thames and Hudson, London, 2009)

Jenkins, Roy, *Churchill* (Macmillan, London, 2001)

Loewenstein, Dora, Dodd, Philip and Watts, Charlie (Eds), *According to the Rolling Stones* (Weidenfeld and Nicolson, London, 2003)

Lyle, Marjorie, *Canterbury, 2000 Years of History* (History Press, Stroud, 1994)

MacGregor, Neil, *A History of The World in 100 Objects* (Allen Lane, London, 2010)

Marsh, Patricia, *The Enigma of the Shell Grotto* (Martyrs Field Publications, Canterbury, 2011)

Maxwell-Stuart, P.G., *Archbishops of Canterbury* (Tempus, Stroud, 2006)

Martin, Graham, *From Vision to Reality, The Making of the University of Kent at Canterbury*, (Eyre and Spottiswood, London, 1990)

McGilchrist, Iain, *The Master and the Emissary, The Divided Brain and the Making of the Western World* (Yale University Press, London, 2009)

McNay, Michael, *Hidden Treasures of England* (Random House, London, 2009)

Mee, Arthur, *Kent* (Hodder and Stoughton, London, 1936)

Moody, Gerald, *The Isle of Thanet, from Prehistory to Norman Conquest* (History Press, Stroud, 2008)

Nicolson, Adam, *Sissinghurst* (Harper Collins, London, 2008)

Nicolson, Nigel, *Portrait of a Marriage* (Weidenfeld and Nicolson, London, 1973)

Nicolson, Nigel (Ed), *Vita and Harold: The Letters of Vita Sackville-West and Harold Nicolson* (Weidenfeld and Nicolson, London, 1992)

North, J.A. (Ed), *The Religious History of The Roman Empire* (Oxford University Press, 2011)

Ogley, Bob, *The Kent Weather Book* (Froglets Publications, 1997)

Paine, David, *The Zborowski Inheritance* (Word-power Books, Edinburgh, 2008)

Philp, Eric, *Butterflies of Kent* (Kent Field Club, Maidstone, 1993)

Sackville-West, Robert, *Inheritance: Knole and the Sackvilles* (Bloomsbury, London, 2010)

Seabrook, David, *All the Devils Are Here* (Granta, London, 2003)

Seeman, Erik, *The Huron-Wendat Feast of the Dead* (Johns Hopkins University Press, Baltimore, 2011)

Smith, Victor, *Front-Line Kent* (Kent County Council, Maidstone, 2007)

Sooley, Howard, *Derek Jarman's Garden* (Thames and Hudson, London, 1995)

Sounes, Howard, *Heist: the True Story of the World's Biggest Cash Robbery* (Simon and Schuster, London, 2009)

Staunton, Michael (Ed), *The Lives of Thomas Becket* (Manchester University Press, 2001)

Sweetinburgh, Sheila (Ed), *Later Medieval Kent* (Boydell and Brewer, Woodbridge, 2010)

Thomson, Graeme, *Under the Ivy: The story of Kate Bush* (Omnibus, London, 2010)

Tomalin, Claire, *The Invisible Woman* (Viking, London, 1990)

Trewin, Ion, *Alan Clark* (Weidenfeld and Nicolson, London, 2009)

Underwood, Peter, *Ghosts of Kent* (Mereborough, Rainham, 1985)

Williams, John (Ed), *The Archaeology of Kent to AD 800* (Boydell Press, Woodbridge, 2007)

Winfield, Rif, *First Rate: The Great Warships of the Age of Sail* (Seaforth, Barnsley, 2010)

Yourgrau, Palle, *Simone Weil* (Reaktion, London, 2011)

OTHER TITLES IN

THE STRANGEST SERIES

The *Strangest* series has been delighting and enthralling readers for decades with weird, exotic, spooky and baffling tales of the absurd, ridiculous and the bizarre. This range of fascinating books – from Football to London, Rugby to Law and many subjects in between – details the very curious history of each one's funniest, oddest and most compelling characters, locations and events.

9781910232910   9781910232866

GOLF'S
STRANGEST®
ROUNDS

9781910232934

KENT'S
STRANGEST®
TALES

9781910232972

LAW'S
STRANGEST®
CASES

9781910232897

LONDON'S
STRANGEST®
TALES

9781910232880

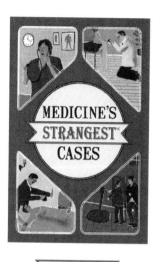

9781910232941

9781910232965

9781910232873

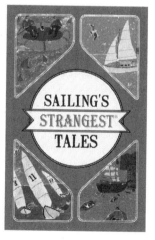

9781911042259

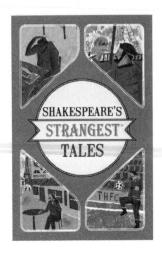

9781910232903

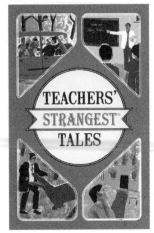

9781910232989

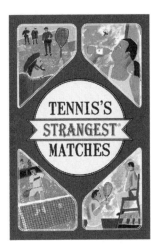

9781910232958